A New Key to the Bible

A New Key to the Bible

*Unlock Its Inner Meaning and Open
the Door to Your Spirit*

BRUCE HENDERSON

**SWEDENBORG
FOUNDATION**
West Chester, Pennsylvania

Library of Congress Cataloging-in-Publication Data
Names: Henderson, Bruce, author.
Title: A new key to the Bible : unlock its inner meaning and open the door to your spirit / Bruce Henderson.
Description: West Chester, Pennsylvania : Swedenborg Foundation, 2018. | Includes bibliographical references.
Identifiers: LCCN 2018019455| ISBN 9780877853084 (pbk. : alk. paper) | ISBN 0877853088 (pbk. : alk. paper)
Subjects: LCSH: Bible--Criticism, interpretation, etc. | New Jerusalem Church--Doctrines. | Swedenborg, Emanuel, 1688-1772.
Classification: LCC BX8726 .H46 2018 | DDC 230/.94--dc23
LC record available at https://lccn.loc.gov/2018019455

Edited by Morgan Beard
Design and typesetting by Karen Connor

Printed in the United States of America

Swedenborg Foundation
320 North Church Street
West Chester, PA 19380
swedenborg.com

To our grandchildren—
Jack and Normandie,
Chyler and Cade,
and Thatcher

I still have many things to say to you, but you cannot bear them now. When the Spirit of truth comes, he will guide you into all the truth. — John 16:12–13

Later on, as I came closer to the building, I saw an inscription above the door: *Now It Is Allowed [Nunc Licet]*, which means that we are now allowed to use our intellect to explore the mysteries of faith. — *True Christianity* §508:3

CONTENTS

ACKNOWLEDGMENTS

Heartfelt love, gratitude, and appreciation to my wife, Carol, for her loving support, counsel, and guidance in preparing this book. She offered steadfast encouragement throughout the process, provided wise editing suggestions, and is a better promoter than I could ever be.

I am always indebted to my late parents, the Rev. Cairns and Eva Henderson, for showing me the way, putting me on the path, and inspiring me to share the insights into God's Word as revealed through Emanuel Swedenborg.

I also owe great thanks to many ministers, teachers, and friends who offered ideas, examples, insights, and resources, often without being aware that they were doing so.

Writing a book like this is an exercise in humility. Anything good that we have to offer to the world really comes from God. Thanks and praise always be to him.

INTRODUCTION

For nothing is hidden that will not be disclosed, nor is anything
secret that will not become known and come to light.
— Luke 8:17

The year 2011 marked the four-hundredth anniversary of the publication of the most popular book in the English language, the King James Version of the Bible. There are more than a billion copies of the book in print, and it still leads the best-seller lists every year. Throughout much of the world, it remains the focus of faith, wonder, doubt, mystery, the search for meaning in life—and controversy.

It took seven years of painstaking labor by forty-seven of the most learned men of England to produce that first edition in 1611. King James's commitment to give "the Word of God" back to the people was revolutionary. His gift not only has left an indelible mark on history, but it has had an enormous influence on English language, literature, and culture.

The King James Bible was proclaimed the official standard of Anglican Christianity and was expected to end the disputes that had grown up around previous English translations. But the Bible remains to this day subject to study, analysis, questioning, and interpretation—more than any other book in history. It is a touchstone for believers, but it is ignored and even attacked by others. Many readers find within the Bible blissful peace and purpose for their lives. Some people fight wars in its name. Others see mysteries and long for explanations. And some don't see anything holy or meaningful in it at all.

During the observance of that four-hundredth anniversary of the King James Version, a reporter for *The Philadelphia Inquirer* praised it as "a mighty collection of wisdom, holiness and comfort—a warning against extremism in religion and secular life."

This prompted a scornful letter from a reader wondering if the reporter had been

> so caught up in the language and translation that [he] missed all the violence: the jealous God full of wrath and vengeance; the genocide; the denigration of women; the approbation of slavery; and the approval of incest and infanticide? Extremism to the max! Most of us are taught to revere the Bible, not read it. When I actually did read it, I became an atheist.

That reader's reaction is far from unique. Thomas Paine (1737–1809), rabble-rouser for the American Revolution, was fiery in condemning the literal words of the Bible in his 1794 book *The Age of Reason:*

> Whenever we read the obscene stories, the voluptuous debaucheries, the cruel and torturous executions, the unrelenting vindictiveness, with which more than half the Bible is filled, it would be more consistent that we called it the word of a demon, than the Word of God. It is a history of wickedness, that has served to corrupt and brutalize mankind; and, for my own part, I sincerely detest it, as I detest everything that is cruel.

François Voltaire (1694–1778), a French author and cynic, proclaimed Christianity a sham and predicted it would be extinct within a hundred years. But within just fifty years of his death, his own house and printing press were used to produce and distribute Bibles in many languages as Christianity thrived.

Most Christians do find comfort and meaning in the Bible, even if they don't grasp every nuance. But why is it often hard to understand? Why is there so much violence and anger? Where is the all-loving, merciful God—especially in the Old Testament? Why did

Jesus make it difficult for people to really know him? Why did he say to his disciples, when they asked why he spoke in parables, "To you it has been given to know the secrets of the kingdom of heaven, but to them it has not been given" (Matthew 13:11)?

Skeptics and believers alike ponder such mysteries as:

- Did God really create the earth in just six days, as is written in Genesis, and then rest on the seventh? How do we reconcile the description there with the physical limits of science? How do we explain it at all?

- Did Noah really gather animals two by two into an ark and ride out a forty-day flood that God allowed to destroy every-one and everything else on earth?

- Why did the children of Israel have to wander for forty years in the wilderness, eating nothing but manna, before reaching the Promised Land?

- Do all those fearful images in Revelation foretell an apocalyptic judgment or the peace of "a new heaven and a new earth"? What does it all mean?

- What do all the stories, people, wars, and images of the Bible have to teach us about who God is? And how does it all relate to our own lives?

Even people who love and revere the Bible often don't agree on what it means, but most of them believe it is either divinely writ-ten or divinely inspired. Even if they don't understand everything, they believe that being open to it as God's Word helps them to grow spiritually. For a believer, the Bible helps to frame the great questions of life: Who is God? How can I get to know him and relate to him? How can reading the Bible give purpose and mean-ing to my life? How can I use it as a guidebook for my own spiri-tual journey?

Indeed, how should any of us read and regard the Bible? Should every word be taken literally, or just figuratively? Is all that ancient context really relevant to our lives? Could there be deeper meaning hidden within its teachings? How will we ever know?

Dan Brown, who beguiled millions of readers with *The Da Vinci Code* and *Angels and Demons,* offered his take on the mysteries of the Bible in another best-seller, *The Lost Symbol.* Here, his popular protagonist, Harvard symbologist Robert Langdon, careens around Washington, DC, probing the mysteries of the Masons in search of this "lost symbol." It turns out to be the "Lost Word," which is buried in the cornerstone of the Washington Monument.

Concealed within the pages of this "Lost Word," Brown writes, "there lies a wondrous secret" (Brown 2009, 487). This, he says, is the lost wisdom of the ancients—the internal meaning of the Bible. Langdon learns that "for America's Masonic forefathers, the Word has been the Bible. And yet few people in history have understood its true message" (487). In this lost ancient book are hidden, powerful secrets, "a vast collection of untapped wisdom waiting to be unveiled" (489).

In Brown's fictional account, once people began separating themselves from God and turning away from him—which is recorded throughout the Bible and all of human history—the true meaning of the Word was lost. One character observes that the ancients who knew that inner meaning would be horrified if they could see how their teachings had been perverted, "how religion has established itself as a tollbooth for heaven. . . . We've lost the Word, and yet its true meaning is still within reach, right before our eyes" (492).

Although Brown's novel was written for entertainment purposes, throughout history there have been thinkers speculating along similar lines. For example, the physicist Isaac Newton (1643–1727) wrote more than a million words on biblical topics, all unpublished during his lifetime, including speculation on the hidden meaning behind the literal words of the Bible.

Emanuel Swedenborg, a well-respected eighteenth-century philosopher and theologian, claimed that he had been given an advantage by God himself. Following an experience of spiritual awakening in his mid-fifties, he described being granted the ability to speak with angels in the spiritual world who explained the spiritual meaning beneath the literal text of the Bible.

So who was Swedenborg? Emanuel Swedenborg (1688–1772) was hailed in his native Sweden and throughout Europe as one of the foremost scientists and intellects of his time. At age fifty-nine, he put aside a prestigious career in science and public service, believing he had received a unique calling from God.

He devoted the last twenty-five years of his life to intense study of the Bible. This resulted in twenty-five volumes of closely reasoned doctrine and descriptions of encounters in the spiritual world, all aimed at giving people a new way of understanding themselves and the world around them. These books include new teachings about God, heaven and hell, true married love, divine providence, and the internal meaning of the Bible.

Swedenborg explains that the spiritual meaning is not readily seen in the literal words alone, just as the soul is invisible in the body. These meanings need to be uncovered or revealed. Think of how you really get to know someone when you get a sense of "the real person" within. Think of a church or school, where the spirit or soul within gives it life and meaning. So it is also, Swedenborg says, with the literal and internal meanings of the Bible. Picture the Bible as a geode: it presents rough stone on the outside, but once opened it glitters with the light and color of a myriad hidden crystals. This is what Swedenborg offers—seeing the Bible in a new light.

Swedenborg insisted that these were not his own theories and interpretations but that everything he wrote came to him from God. The reception among his peers was mixed. Some were intrigued and others were welcoming, but some clergy and scholars were intensely critical. It is natural and healthy to approach any claim to revelation with skepticism, and Swedenborg was ready for this. But learned people did begin to take notice of his books, and eventually a church developed around them, beginning in England. More than two hundred years later, this church has spread throughout the world, although it still is relatively small.

His books were widely read and appreciated among intellectuals of the nineteenth century. Ralph Waldo Emerson called him "a colossal soul who lies vast abroad on his times. He is not to be measured by whole colleges of ordinary scholars" (Emerson 1930, 102–3). Elizabeth Barrett Browning said of Swedenborg's revelation, "It explains much that was incomprehensible" (Kenyon 1898, 34). And in the twentieth century, Helen Keller, a devoted reader of Swedenborg throughout her life, called him "an eye among the blind, and ear among the deaf" and "one of the noblest champions Christianity has ever known" (Keller 1953, 17, 25).

The introduction to Helen Keller's *How I Would Help the World* states that "it was Swedenborg's teachings, more than anything else, that helped her to understand, accept, and transcend her limitations." It goes on to quote her as saying that his message "has given color and reality and unity to my thought of the life to come; it has exalted my ideas of love, truth and usefulness; it has been my strongest incitement to overcome limitations" (Keller 2011, 11).

Swedenborg never tried to attract attention to himself, establish an institutional church, or even gather a following. He published his books anonymously until his authorship became known. He humbly described himself as "a servant of the Lord." There is a Church of the New Jerusalem, or simply "New Church," which has grown up around these teachings; its members do not consider themselves followers of Swedenborg, but rather of the doctrines given through him.

Whether or not you believe that what Swedenborg wrote was divine, he offers a fresh opportunity for anyone, no matter how skeptical, to seek deeper meanings within scripture. He uses the principle of correspondences (see chapter 1) to reveal an internally consistent, verse-by-verse interpretation of the Bible that ultimately points the way to our own spiritual growth.

For example, one of the most challenging books of the Bible is Revelation, with all its mystifying symbols and apocalyptic scenes. One of the many strange images in John's vision is of a book sealed with seven seals. The literal description of what happens as each seal is opened is still mysterious: four horsemen on red, white, black, and pale horses; white robes washed in the blood of the Lamb; souls huddled under an altar, praying for help; and a massive earthquake that turns the sun black and the moon as red as blood.

In his explanation of all of this, Swedenborg describes a spiritual judgment in which God looks inside each person to see the quality of their faith and the way that they lived their lives. He emphasizes that faith is not real faith at all if it is divorced from loving others and putting that love into action in everything we do. Though there is turbulence through the process of opening the seals, when the seventh and last seal is opened, there is complete silence in heaven. Swedenborg says this signifies that the angels were amazed at all that had gone on before. Then seven angels blow seven trumpets, representing divine love and wisdom flowing into the world and into each individual. This is the precursor to the final stage, when a new age of spiritual understanding—the New Jerusalem—comes into being.

Dan Brown's books have been both acclaimed and reviled, but they are generally popular because readers love drama and a search for truth—and they love a good story. The Bible is also filled with drama, good stories, and mystery about what it all means. Many of Brown's fans may resonate with the idea that there must be a deeper meaning to the often-cryptic words of the Bible, the "lost symbols" of the ancients just waiting to be rediscovered. Maybe we don't need a heroic professor and a page-turning tale of danger and intrigue to uncover that meaning. Now we can explore and judge for ourselves Swedenborg's claim that he has the key to reveal the hidden, spiritual meanings within the Bible.

A New Key to the Bible

1

A WHOLE NEW LIGHT ON THE BIBLE

The Bible gives me a deep, comforting sense that things seen are temporal, and things unseen are eternal.

Helen Keller

I am busily engaged in the study of the Bible. I believe it is God's word because it finds me where I am.

— Abraham Lincoln

The Bible grows more beautiful as we grow in our understanding of it.

— Johann Wolfgang von Goethe

Many of us grew up knowing something about the biblical stories of David and Goliath, Jonah and the whale, and Daniel in the lion's den, just as we grew up with the "once upon a time" myths and legends of fairy tales.

Children love stories that pit good against evil, with heroes and heroines, dragons and witches, and monsters and fairies. From Snow White to Harry Potter and *The Lord of the Rings* to *Star Wars*, we are drawn in by our imagination. Reading about the trials and adventures of others, we may even begin to sense conflict within ourselves—between a darker, selfish nature and more loving, caring instincts.

This mirroring plays out as well in our reading of the Bible. Christians may catch glimpses of themselves in Moses, Mary, David, and the disciple Peter—and even in such less-admirable characters as Herod, Job, and Jezebel. As we become aware that people are not all good or bad but know something of both in their lives, we gain insight into the complexity of our own inner nature and the choices that we make every day. We've probably known something of the dark and scary dragon's lair and the bright promise of Cinderella's fairy godmother. Similarly, images in the Bible can be terrifying—like the dragon ready to devour the child of the woman clothed with the sun (Revelation 12:4)—or uplifting, like the vision of heaven descending to earth (Revelation 21:2).

The repetition of stories like these, whether in fairy tales or in the Bible, and how we process them help to form character and conscience. This is what Emanuel Swedenborg calls the Bible's purpose: teaching us to know God; to recognize what is true and good; to develop spiritual conscience; and to find peace in happy, useful lives that lead to heaven.

For many people, the familiar stories and parables in the Bible live in their imaginations and speak simple truths. There are layers for children, like fables with morals. There are layers for adults through which we may recognize destructive behavior, such as David sending Bathsheba's husband to his death so that he could take her for his own wife. And there are hints of deeper spiritual layers, such as the persistent trials and lessons of the children of Israel. But it is not just the parables that have spiritual meanings: every word of the Bible does—even the dry listings of laws and genealogies, the descriptions of bloody wars, and the depictions of corrupt people.

Swedenborg teaches, for instance, that the first eleven books of Genesis, which include the garden of Eden, Adam and Eve, Noah, the Flood, and the Tower of Babel, are divine allegories, not meant to be taken literally. The real meaning is in the symbolism, not in the historical record. That does not diminish them, though; it enriches them, with their spiritual meaning lifting them out of ancient context into compelling relevance for our own lives.

This is the way God teaches, Swedenborg asserts: not with straightforward lessons but through parables that we have to work at to understand completely. "Jesus told the crowds all these things in parables; without a parable he told them nothing" (Matthew 13:34). The Bible—from Genesis to Revelation—can be seen as one continuous parable about our own lives, with layers of meaning hidden in the text.

Swedenborg assures us that

> within the Word, in *every single part,* there is a spiritual sense, which deals with the Lord's kingdom; and within that internal sense there is the Divine, since the Word in its inmost sense deals with the Lord alone. This is the source and holiness and life of the Word; it derives them from no other source. (*Secrets of Heaven* §8943)

The key to accessing this spiritual sense is what he describes as a "language of correspondence" between the material world and the spiritual world. In perhaps his best-known work, *Heaven and Hell,* Swedenborg addresses just what correspondences are.

> The whole natural world is responsive to the spiritual world—
> the natural world not just in general, but in detail. So whatever
> arises in the natural world out of the spiritual one is called
> "something that corresponds." It needs to be realized that
> the natural world arises from and is sustained in being by the
> spiritual world, exactly the way an effect relates to its efficient
> cause. . . .
>
> We can see in the human face what correspondence is like.
> In a face that has not been taught to dissimulate, all the affec-
> tions of the mind manifest themselves visibly in a natural form,
> as though in their very imprint, which is why we refer to the face
> as "the index of the mind." This is our spiritual world within our
> natural world. Similarly, elements of our understanding are man-
> ifest in our speech, and matters of our volition in our physical
> behavior. So things that occur in the body, whether in our faces
> or in our speech or in our behavior, are called correspondences.
> (*Heaven and Hell* §§89, 91)

Here Swedenborg uses an example most of us have experienced in daily life: the expression on a person's face reflects what's
happening in his or her mind. In the same way, he explains, what
happens in our world reflects what's happening in the spiritual
realms of heaven, hell, and the world of spirits in between. When
interpreting the Bible, he describes how certain objects, actions, and
even people's names can reflect a deeper spiritual dynamic, one that
is constantly at work in world events and in our own lives. He uses
correspondences to give new meaning to stories that don't seem to
make logical sense or to details that appear insignificant.

Swedenborg explains, for instance, that every number mentioned
in the Bible has a correspondence. The number three means full-
ness, or completeness. Think of the trinity of Father, Son, and Holy
Spirit within one God; or of the mind, body, and soul within each
of us. Every animal or bird and every person, place, and thing mentioned in the Bible has a correspondence that enriches its meaning.

Many of these correspondences are readily apparent and make sense. For instance, Swedenborg says, the ear corresponds to obedience, as in "Give ear to my words" (Psalm 5:1). Rocks, stones, and water correspond to truth: "On this rock I will build my church" (Matthew 16:18), and "Those who drink of the water that I will give them will never be thirsty" (John 4:14). And think of the parable of the wise and foolish builders from Matthew 7:24–27: the houses built upon rock (truth) and sand (false doctrine) both suffered the storms of wind and rain, but only the house built on the foundation of truth remained standing.

The story of the young shepherd David defeating the giant warrior Goliath with nothing more than a stone and a slingshot is a simple, heroic tale of innocent good overcoming monstrous evil. But the internal sense adds a new level of meaning. Goliath represents his people's pride in their own intelligence and the false ideas that that pride led them to believe. David chooses five smooth stones from a stream for his sling—remember that rocks and stones stand for truth—and the number five, Swedenborg says, corresponds to a little bit, or a sufficient amount.

We may never have to face down a giant Goliath, but some issues in our lives can seem overwhelming. God wants us to know that if we follow him, we can always find "five smooth stones"—enough truth and principles—to fight against our wayward inclinations and to be loving toward others. Goliath stands for the corruption of truth. He can loom large in our lives, Swedenborg says, but he can be brought down by using the simple truths we get from God. Even a little bit of truth can destroy a false idea.

Among the more challenging stories of the Bible for believers to understand and reconcile are those depicting an angry, cruel, and vengeful God. Consider the story from Joshua 8, where Joshua and the Israelites are commanded by God to destroy the city of Ai and all its inhabitants. God said to Joshua, "Stretch out the sword that is in your hand toward Ai; for I will give it into your hand" (18). And Joshua did just that "until he had utterly destroyed all the inhabitants of Ai" (26). He and his army ambushed and killed twelve thousand men, women, and children; set fire to the city; and made it "forever a heap of ruins, as it is to this day" (28).

How could God command that something be done that is so contrary to his nature—the slaughter of people and the wanton destruction of their city?

In the spiritual meaning, the men of Ai represent the evil or purely worldly ideas within us; the women represent the worldly things we love; and the children represent what we reap from such desires. So God was not actually ordering the brutal killing of innocent men, women, and children, Swedenborg contends, but was showing us how to rid ourselves of the selfish things we do and love in our own lives. The literal meaning of this story may seem alien to us and to our concept of God, but Swedenborg is teaching that the spiritual sense reveals the true nature of God and the Bible and that it can add meaning to our lives.

In other cases, it's not one's concept of God that seems at odds with the biblical text; rather, science tells us that some of the things described in the Bible cannot be literally true—for example, the story of Creation in Genesis. Many people take this account of the seven days of Creation as a miracle that does not need to conform to rational limits. Others might see it as an ancient myth. Swedenborg offers a different perspective: that in the internal sense of the Bible, these six days can be seen as the ongoing story of our own individual "creation"—the growth and development of our mind and character through six distinct days, or stages, in our lives. This is what is meant, he says, by separating light from darkness (the dawn of our rationality) or by the earth bringing forth fruit (the good things we do in our lives). A deeper understanding of the Bible doesn't take anything away from the comfort that many people draw from the literal words, but it can enlighten them and even help to confirm and magnify their faith.

The reason why the "soul" of the Bible had been hidden for all those centuries, Swedenborg says, is that the spiritual meaning of the words had been lost. In various works, he describes the spiritual history of the human race. In the earliest times, he says, people lived in such close harmony with God that they instinctively understood and even perceived the world in correspondences.

> I have been taught that the people of the earliest [spiritual age], the one that existed before the Flood, were so heavenly in nature that they talked with angels of heaven, and that they were able to talk with them in correspondences. This meant that their wisdom developed to the point that when they saw anything on earth, they not only thought of it in earthly terms but thought of it in spiritual terms at the same time, and therefore their thoughts joined those of angels.
>
> I have also been taught that Enoch (mentioned in Genesis 5:21–24) and others who joined him collected correspondences from the mouth of these [sages] and passed their knowledge on to their descendants. As a result of this, the knowledge of correspondences was not only familiar but was devotedly practiced in many Middle Eastern countries, especially in the land of Canaan, Egypt, Assyria, Chaldea, Syria, and Arabia; and in Tyre, Sidon, and Nineveh. From coastal locations it was transmitted to Greece. There, however, the knowledge was changed into fables, as we can tell from the writings of the earliest people there. (*Sacred Scripture* §21)

It could be something out of one of Dan Brown's novels: ancient people being attuned to these correspondences and able to decipher the deeper meaning within them, an ability that was gradually lost over time as people became less spiritual. In fact, when Swedenborg refers to the Bible as "the Word," he is not restricting it to just the Bible. The Word, he says, actually refers to any sacred scripture or set of teachings with an internal sense. For Christians, it's the Bible, but Swedenborg mentions that the Word has existed among other people as well. Indeed, as Swedenborg writes in the same volume:

> Do you think that the ancient sages including Aristotle, Cicero, Seneca, and others who wrote about God and the immortality of the soul picked this up first from themselves? No, it was from

others, who had it handed down to them from still others who first learned it from the Word. (*Sacred Scripture* §115:3)

Wherever it appears, the Word is always written in this language of correspondences, because this is how God himself communicates—from the spiritual plane of heaven down into our natural world. The chapters that follow will explore how correspondences can give us a new perspective on such familiar tales as Adam and Eve, Noah and the Ark, and the story of Moses, as well as on the New Testament accounts of Jesus's life on earth and the bizarre imagery in Revelation.

Everything in the Bible not only is holy and spiritually meaningful, but it also speaks to our own lives. Swedenborg wants us to see these stories of people and events from thousands of years ago as still intensely relevant to us today. By holding up both the literal and internal meanings of the Bible as a mirror for our experiences, Swedenborg invites us to see ourselves and our struggles within scripture and to find there a path to peace and happiness.

2

IN THE BEGINNING . . .

The Bible shows how the world progresses. It begins with a garden, but ends with a holy city.

— Phillip Brooks

When you read God's Word, you must constantly be saying to yourself, "It is talking to me, and about me."

— Søren Kierkegaard

While I know myself as a creation of God, I am also obligated to realize and remember that everyone else and everything else are also God's creation.

— Maya Angelou

I t all starts right at the beginning of the Bible, in the story of Creation.

The literal reading of Genesis 1 encompasses darkness and light, seas and dry land, vegetation and animals, and human beings created in God's image. Swedenborg tells us that the biblical story of Creation is not about the physical beginning of the world—the transformation from a void in space into a living earth—but about the creation and rebirth of each one of us. It is the growth we experience through six "days," or stages, of our spiritual lives. The story is one that speaks to us about how God guides us through each step of our spiritual development.

In the Gospel of John, Jesus tells Nicodemus that "no one can see the kingdom of God without being born from above." On the literal level, this is a strange statement. Nicodemus understandably asks, "How can anyone be born after having grown old? Can one enter a second time into the mother's womb and be born?" Jesus answers, "Very truly, I tell you, no one can enter the kingdom of God without being born of water and Spirit. What is born of the flesh is flesh, and what is born of the Spirit is spirit. Do not be astonished that I said to you, 'You must be born from above'" (3:3, 4, 5–7).

The entire Bible can be read from a historical perspective, Swedenborg says, but on a deeper level it is really all about our individual journey from birth to rebirth—being *born from above,* or "born again," as a person destined for heaven. His word for this type of spiritual rebirth is *regeneration,* a lifelong process of changing the way we think, understand, and act. This process is all about shunning evil, choosing good, and focusing on God and heaven rather than on ourselves and the material world. Regeneration is at work through the trials and temptations of life and also through the choices we make every day.

In the beginning, we are born in darkness and ignorance. As we progress through life, we make the choices that determine our true character. Swedenborg cautions that not everyone reaches the final stage—the seventh day, when the struggles are over and the lessons are learned—in this world. Most people progress through only the first few days of re-creation. But he also describes an afterlife where those who truly want to become good and loving people can continue growing and learning, even after they have entered heaven.

Day One

In the beginning, God created heaven and earth. And the earth was void and emptiness; and there was darkness on the face of the abyss. And the Spirit of God was constantly moving on the face of the water. And God said, "Let there be light," and there was light. And God saw the light, that it was good; and God made a distinction between light and darkness. . . . And there was evening and there was morning, the first day. (Genesis 1:1–4, 5 [*Secrets of Heaven,* p. 7])

The first day describes the initial stage of our spiritual development. It starts at infancy and continues until we begin the process of regeneration by consciously choosing to live good lives, rejecting behavior that is selfish or harmful to others (in other words, evil). Some people may live their entire lives without moving past this first stage.

The earliest we can start growing spiritually is in adolescence, when our conscience develops to the point that we can distinguish between right and wrong and make rational choices to do one or the other. A newborn baby is full of promise and delight, but those things are only potential. The child comes into the world knowing nothing, completely dependent on his or her parents. Soon the child begins growing and learning, emerging from ignorance and darkness into light and awareness. It is a joy to witness, but for the child, the process is full of trials. There is a long journey involved—learning to walk and talk; years of schooling, correction, and direction; slowly becoming an adult. Throughout all of this early development, God is nurturing our spiritual progress.

We begin our lives in a spiritual void, with no understanding or awareness of goodness or truth. The *face of the abyss* describes the worldly things that attract us and any false ideas we cling to. This Bible passage goes on to tell us that God is working secretly within each of us, guiding us to the next phase of our spiritual lives—if we choose to follow the inner voice that urges us toward good. It is God's spirit that is *moving on the face of the water.*

We can't really learn what is true and do what is good in God's eyes until we give up our old ways so that we can be reborn—when we "see the light." This is the *distinction between light and darkness:* the growing awareness of the difference between God's goodness and truth and the self-indulgence that comes from our own ego. It is the dawning awareness that there is nothing good and true in the world except what comes from God.

We hear this same wisdom reflected in John:

> In the beginning there was the Word, and the Word was present with God, and the Word was God. Everything was made by him, and nothing that was made was made without him. In him was life, and the life was the light of humankind; but the light appears in the darkness. He was the true light that shines on every person coming into the world. (1:1, 3–5, 9 [*Secrets of Heaven* §20])

The right path may at times seem simple and clear and at other times shadowy, but in the light we see our life for what it is. Without that perspective, it's easy to fall prey to the illusion that we can do it all on our own. When the light begins to dawn, Swedenborg says, we see that we need to trust the guidance of the Spirit of God within us.

This first day is a prolonged stage in our life. As we advance, we waken to the morning light from out of the darkness of living without faith. God is preparing our hearts to be awakened to spiritual life. That is when we see the light and know that *it is good.*

Day Two

And God said, "Let there be an expanse in the middle of the
waters, and let it exist to make a distinction among the waters, in
the waters." And God made the expanse, and he made a distinction between the waters that were under the expanse and the
waters that were over the expanse; and so it was done. And God
called the expanse heaven. And there was evening and there was
morning, the second day. (Genesis 1:6–8 [*Secrets of Heaven*, p. 7])

The second stage divides. It separates what is God's, such as goodness and truth, from what is our own, with all the cares and anxiet-
ies of the world. This doesn't happen without struggle, as the word
division implies.

This stage in our spiritual growth begins with an awakening to
the realization that there is a God, a being higher than ourselves.
The part of us that comes to this realization, the *expanse* described
in the verses above, is our inner self.

Before we are reborn, we have no idea about the spiritual and
natural dimensions within us. We are absorbed with the world, with
everything we see and experience. We may be good people, trying to be honest and to do what is right, but there is a difference
between understanding the rules of morality that we are taught and
doing good because we truly care about other people.

At this stage, then, we distinguish between the things that are
spiritual and the things that are of this world. This is the *distinction
among the waters* described in the verses above. The understanding
that comes from the inner self—from our spiritual connection to
the Divine—is what is meant by the *waters over the expanse,* while
the facts about nature that we have learned are the *waters under the
expanse.*

If we allow God to help us grow spiritually, we may develop a
new sense of awareness, begin to see purpose on a higher plane in
life, and set our priorities accordingly. As we listen to conscience, we
may confess, atone, make resolutions, and vow to better ourselves.
And as we are drawn to spiritual truth, our future brightens.

Swedenborg tells us that God will use the things that we love, the things that we most enjoy doing in this world, to lead us toward a more spiritual life. That is why the expanse where our spiritual and worldly sides meet—our inner self—is called *heaven.*

Day Three

And God said, "Let the waters under heaven be gathered into one place, and let dry land appear," and so it was done. And God called the dry land earth, and the gathering of waters he called seas. And God saw that it was good. And God said, "Let the earth cause the sprouting on the earth of the tender plant, of the plant bearing its seed, of the fruit tree making the fruit that holds its seed, each in the way of its kind," and so it was done. . . . And God saw that it was good. And there was evening and there was morning, the third day. (Genesis 1:9–11, 12–13 [*Secrets of Heaven,* p. 7])

The third stage is the beginning of repentance. The awareness of our inner self that was created in the previous stage has taken root in our everyday mind. Now we are aware that there have been times when we made bad choices, when we hurt others; and we resolve to do better. The gathered waters mentioned in the verses above are our collected knowledge and experience, both spiritual and secular, which are stored in our memory. Our conscious mind is the *dry land,* or *earth,* ready to receive the seeds from God to make our lives useful and productive—to bear fruit.

We don't go from self-centered to spiritual overnight. As our focus shifts to other people, we might find ourselves doing small things for others—helping someone who's struggling to carry a heavy load, for example, or giving someone a ride even though we're in a hurry and it's out of our way. This is the *tender plant,* the small act of kindness that represents a fragile new life within us. Next comes the *seed-bearing plant,* the action that not only helps others but allows for good deeds to spread. Instead of just contributing to a food drive, now we're organizing one where it never existed before. We not only donate to a good cause, but we encourage our friends to do the same. Then comes the *fruit tree,* the action that continues to bear fruit all on its own. Maybe we help to build a house for someone in need, or we start a charitable organization that will continue long after our involvement ends.

This is when the self-confidence of making our own decisions may give way to humility—we may have achieved material success, but have we made a real, positive impact on the world? Have we truly taken care of the people we love and been considerate to strangers in need? When we allow God to plant seeds in our lives and guide their growth, it gives us the ability to see the bigger picture.

We see this theme repeated in the Gospels. In the parable of the sower (Matthew 13:1–9, Mark 4:3–9, and Luke 8:4–8), Jesus describes a man who sets out to plant seeds by scattering them all over. In the story, the seeds represent the words of God. Whether the seeds land on the wayside, in stony places, among thorns, or on good ground is all about the state of our own mind. But we tend not to be aware of this.

> So God's kingdom is like one who tosses seed into the earth and sleeps and rises night and day, and the seed sprouts and grows; how it happens, the person does not know. For the earth bears fruit readily—first a shoot, then an ear, then the full grain in the ear. (Mark 4:26, 27, 28 [*Secrets of Heaven* §29:2])

This third day of Creation is really about the kingdom of God— the love and goodness and truth of the Divine—being planted within each one of us. "God's kingdom does not come in an observable way, nor will they say, 'Look here!' or 'Look there!' because— look!—God's kingdom is within you" (Luke 17:20, 21 [*Secrets of Heaven* §29:2]).

Even if we just have the dimmest idea of heaven within us, as we experience moments of peace and joy, this is the beginning of gaining a new life. And as we continue to advance from darkness and shadow to light, this is when we begin to change the way we look at the world.

Day Four

And God said, "Let there be lights in the expanse of the heavens to make a distinction between day and night...." And God made the two great lights: the greater light to rule by day and the smaller light to rule by night; and the stars. (Genesis 1:14, 16 [*Secrets of Heaven*, p. 7])

The fourth stage of our re-creation is a turning point. Just as a new light came into the world, we begin to see our lives in a new light through the love and faith we receive from God.

The first three stages—the first three days—are similar to going to school, learning, and discovering and storing up knowledge from the world. During those stages, our faith is based first on facts that are given to us and then on our intellect, which we use to sift through information and choose what to accept as true. In this fourth stage, faith finally comes from the heart. It is faith born of love toward others. And this, Swedenborg says, is true faith.

Love is the key to this process. According to Swedenborg, the *greater light* in the sky represents love, while the *smaller light* is faith. The love described here is divine love, which is the source of life itself. Swedenborg tells us that nothing is alive unless it is animated by God's love, just as no action is truly good unless it is motivated by love. In the third stage, our good deeds were motivated by an intellectual faith that was based on what we learned as children about being good members of society. In the fourth stage, a genuine love toward others blooms inside us; we do what's right because we really want to, not because we feel as though we should. The lights are placed on the *expanse of the heavens,* or our inner self—where divine love first enters into us—and then the light shines from us out into the world.

The lights of love and faith come equally to everyone, as does the sun's light and warmth. We are always free to decide whether to let these lights lead us in our lives. The more that people are selfish and caught up in the cares of the world, the more that they are apt to turn away from God and from loving or serving their neighbors. On the other hand, the more that people let divine love and faith into their hearts, the easier it becomes to choose good. And with this openness toward God, our spiritual re-creation continues.

Day Five

And God said, "Let the waters cause the creeping animal—a living soul—to creep out. And let the bird flit over the land, over the face of the expanse of the heavens." And God created the big sea creatures, and every living, creeping soul that the waters caused to creep out, in all their kinds, and every bird on the wing, of every kind. And God saw that it was good. And God blessed them, saying, "Reproduce and multiply and fill the water in the seas, and the birds will multiply on the land." (Genesis 1:20–22 [*Secrets of Heaven*, p. 8])

One of the lessons from the last stage was that nothing is truly alive unless it is animated by God's love. As we allow that love to flow into us, we enter the fifth stage, which is when we truly become spiritually alive. Life becomes richer and more meaningful, because we aren't trying to live from our own power and then dealing with the fallout of our egotistical choices. Instead, we are sustained by the unlimited power of God's love within us.

We progress from the tender plants of the third day to birds and animals—called *living souls*—that symbolize a new understanding of faith. We aren't dependent on what others tell us to believe. We observe and reason: we understand the spiritual principles involved, and we confirm it for ourselves by watching the positive effects that ripple outward from our actions.

In these verses, too, we can see some specific examples of correspondences. According to Swedenborg, *birds* represent logical reasoning, *fish* represent facts, and the *big sea creatures* represent broad categories of knowledge. A person at this stage has wisdom, but it is a human wisdom, which is derived from life experience. The transcendence of divine wisdom comes in later stages.

In these verses, to *reproduce* and *multiply* means to spread the fruits of loving, spiritual acts. This is a process that starts with the things that we do and then spreads far beyond our range of influence.

Everything that starts with life (love) from God reproduces and multiplies beyond anything we can imagine. We get just a glimpse of that not only in the bounty of nature but also in what we do for others, the fruits that we produce through our own labors. Swedenborg assures us that this is nothing compared with what we will experience in the next life, where blessings never end. We can be tremendously useful and productive in this life, but in heaven the opportunities will just keep multiplying.

Day Six

And God said, "Let the earth produce each living soul according to its kind: the beast . . . and the wild animal of the earth, each according to its kind"; and so it was done. . . . And God said, "Let us make a human in our image, after our likeness; and these will rule over the fish of the sea and over the bird in the heavens, and over the beast, and over all the earth. . . ." And God created the human in his image; in God's image he created them; male and female he created them. And God blessed them, and God said to them, "Reproduce and multiply, and fill the earth and harness it, and rule over the fish of the sea and over the bird in the heavens and over every living animal creeping on the earth." And God said, "Here, now, I am giving you every seed-bearing plant on the face of all the earth and every tree that has fruit; the tree that produces seed will serve you for food. And every wild animal of the earth and every bird in the heavens and every animal creeping on the earth, in which there is a living soul—every green plant will serve them for nourishment." And so it was done. (Genesis 1:24, 26, 27–30 [*Secrets of Heaven,* p. 8])

The sixth stage is the culmination of our rebirth, or regeneration— when we replace our old, selfish will with God's; when we do what he loves; and when we live *in his image.* This is when we are ready to enter heaven.

The humanness of God is a theme that Swedenborg repeats over and over throughout his writings. He doesn't mean that God is literally an old man up in the sky, but rather that being human is a matter of having love (life) and acting through wisdom. If we start from the premise that love is life itself, then what could God be except the ultimate source of love? And if we talk about truth and wisdom in terms of the spiritual principles of the universe, then what could God be except the ultimate source of wisdom? In Swedenborg's theology, then, to be human is to be made of love and wisdom; and since God is the greatest universal example of humanity, when we live spiritually, we become true human beings in miniature.

This transition happens during the sixth stage. Instead of acting from intellectual understanding, we truly begin to act out of love. Swedenborg puts it this way:

> In the fifth stage we speak with conviction (an attribute of the intellect) and in the process strengthen ourselves in truth and goodness. The things we then produce have life in them and are called the fish of the sea and the birds in the heavens. And in the sixth stage we act with conviction (an attribute of the intellect) and therefore with love (an attribute of the will) in speaking truth and doing good. What we then produce is called a living soul, an animal. Because this is the point at which we begin to act as much with love as with conviction, we become spiritual people, who are called [God's] image. (*Secrets of Heaven* §48)

When the biblical verses talk about human beings ruling over the animals, the birds, the fish, and the plants, it's really about mastering what those things represent. You can be spiritually enriched by the facts that you've learned, the things that your reason tells you, and the good deeds that you've done; but don't let them overpower your spiritual understanding. For example, you might enjoy learning new things, but a person at this stage knows that the highest purpose of learning is to use that knowledge to help others. And while helping others is a good thing, if you start telling yourself how great a person you are for doing so, then you're putting yourself on the path back to self-centered thinking.

Anyone who has reached this stage still lives and functions as usual but thinks and operates from a higher perspective. Such people have heaven within them, and it shows in their kindness, patience, love, and mercy. However, even at this level of regeneration, our outer nature will fight back against the good impulses coming from our inner nature; and we will still have bad days when frustration, anger, or temptation gets the better of us. Those struggles don't end until the seventh day.

Reaching Day Seven

All six stages of regeneration come with struggle. Just as the children of Israel escaping from slavery in Egypt endured terrible plagues and forty years in the wilderness before coming at last to the Promised Land, we have to break the hold of old habits and cravings that enslave us. That takes time, commitment, and dealing with frustration, but all the while God is trying to raise us up to new levels and strengthen us.

One important lesson of the Creation story is that in times of temptation and internal conflict, God may seem remote; but, in fact, he never is. How often might we feel abandoned and wonder why God lets us endure pain and doubt without his help and comfort? But that is when he is really closest to us. It is like the familiar story of a man walking with God who sees two sets of footprints in the sand. When the man battles his inner demons, there is only one set of footprints, and he asks why God abandoned him. God replies, "That is when I carried you." He never leaves us.

The re-creation, or rebirth, of each of us is a creation process in God's hands, just like the creation of the world. God created us to receive his love, and he wants us to share that love with others through the way we live our lives. We only make it harder on ourselves if we don't choose to work with him. As Swedenborg puts it: "The reason why faith which looks away from the Lord toward self is a loser is that then the person does all the fighting alone" (*Secrets of Heaven* §8606).

Those symbolic six days of Creation represent the six stages we pass through until we become God's image:

- In the first stage, we are in darkness, unaware of spiritual reality and (in some cases) not rationally able to make the choice between good and evil.

- In the second stage, we become aware of the spiritual side of life and the existence of a higher power.

- In the third stage, we understand that we have sometimes acted in harmful ways toward others and, if we want to make amends, begin to act in helpful ways instead.

- In the fourth, those acts of kindness lead to true love and faith stirring within us.

- In the fifth, we have seen that love and faith lead to good things, and we express that to others; but we are still acting from an intellectual understanding.

- In the sixth, we move beyond intellect and act out of true love and compassion for others.

When the conflict is finally over, we can rest in the bliss of the seventh day—the Sabbath—as described in Genesis 2. This is when the struggles end, and people no longer need to make a conscious effort to do good in the world. They simply act out of love and wisdom, with no thought of behaving any differently, because all parts of their mind are in harmony. Embracing the peace of God, the people who reach this state are truly heavenly. They are angels on earth.

However, this is just the first chapter of the first book of the Bible! The Old and New Testaments are filled with stories and situations that relate to us, just as do the struggles and triumphs that play out through these six stages of our spiritual lives. Everything in the Bible speaks to us, but it is all condensed in the Creation story.

And God saw all that he had done and, yes, it was very good.
(Genesis 1:31 [*Secrets of Heaven*, p. 8])

3

"SURELY THE LORD IS IN THIS PLACE"

The Garden of Eden

We must cultivate our own garden. When man was put in the garden of Eden he was put there so that he should work, which proves that man was not born to rest.

— Voltaire

Noah and the Ark

The story of Noah, like other stories in the first 11 chapters of Genesis, are archetypal. Noah's story tells us that human beings have an inherent tendency towards violence, both towards their fellow human beings and towards the creation itself. The story tells us that this violence grieves God.

— Adam Hamilton

The Tower of Babel

As soon as he reflected seriously he was convinced of the existence of God and immortality, and at once he instinctively said to himself, "I want to live for immortality, and I will accept no compromise." In the same way, if he had decided that God and immortality did not exist, he would have at once become an atheist and a socialist. For socialism is not merely the labor question, it is before all things the atheistic question, the question of the form taken by atheism today, the question of the tower of Babel built without God, not to mount to heaven from earth but to set up heaven on earth.

— Fyodor Dostoyevsky, *The Brothers Karamazov*

S wedenborg tells us that the first eleven chapters of Genesis are allegorical, meaning that they are to be understood spiritually rather than literally. He says it does not diminish the story to say that the creation of the universe did not happen in six days or that there was no Adam and Eve, no garden of Eden, no flood covering the earth, no ark, or no Tower of Babel. These parables are important, but their value lies in their spiritual meaning more than in the literal words.

In the previous chapter, we saw how the account of Creation can be seen as the story of our own creation, leading from the moment of our birth until the point when we become divinely loving beings. In Genesis 2, we see this process working in reverse: from a state of bliss and union with the Divine, Adam and Eve separate and move away from God. Their descendants move even further, embracing evil to such an extent that it threatens to wipe out all remnants of good in the world—goodness that is saved when Noah gathers it up in an ark. We see this process at work again in the story of the Tower of Babel, where blind ambition drives humanity to try to become equal to God.

Throughout all of these stories, we see how we ourselves can fall into the trap of self-delusion and egotism, working to promote ourselves at the expense of others. The consequences for us can be just as disastrous as they are for those in Genesis—but there is always the hope of turning things around, if we are willing to trust in a higher power.

Adam and Eve and the Garden of Eden

Adam and Eve. The garden of Eden. The apple. The serpent. The tree of the knowledge of good and evil. Banishment. It is one of the oldest dramas of all time. Swedenborg tells us that the inner meaning of this story has to do with the choices we make. That may seem obvious—we all face the temptation to seek out pleasures (the "apple") that will ultimately harm us. In this case, though, the choice has to do with the way we relate to God.

Gardens, trees, flowers, and plants are common symbols in the Bible, with clear connotations. "I am the vine, you are the branches" (John 15:5). People who trust the Lord are like trees planted by the water (Psalm 1:3). The tents of Israel are like gardens by rivers and like trees that the Lord has planted (Numbers 24:6). In Isaiah, we read: "The Lord will guide you continually, and satisfy your needs in parched places . . . and you shall be like a watered garden, like a spring of water, whose waters never fail" (58:11). If we understand these metaphors as applying to our inner self, we might see that gardens—especially the garden of Eden—are like spiritual states within our minds, where good things grow.

In the previous chapter, we saw that on the seventh day of Creation, which is also the final stage of a person's spiritual growth, the individual experiences a state of rest, a complete cessation of struggle. This state, Swedenborg says, is represented by the garden of Eden. In Eden, all life is sustained by God, and the inhabitants live in complete trust—complete faith—in that source of life.

Swedenborg explains that this was also the state of the earliest people on earth, the people who belonged to the first "church," which you could imagine as the first phase in humanity's collective spiritual evolution. Thus the story of Eden is not only about the fall of two individuals; it is also about the fall of this first church and the beginning of the separation between human beings and the Divine.

The story of the garden of Eden is about people making bad decisions, even after dire warnings, and suffering for them. Swedenborg teaches that it's really about our own intelligence and wisdom and also about the choices we make.

In the Bible, Adam and Eve are warned not to eat from the tree of knowledge of good and evil, for if they do, they will die. They obey at first, until a serpent tempts Eve by telling her that she will not die but instead have her eyes opened so that she will "be like God" (Genesis 3:5).

The key to this story is a concept that first came up in the discussion of Creation. Knowledge is a wonderful thing, but if we rely on the facts we've learned or even the evidence of our senses, it's easy to deceive ourselves or to be influenced in a negative way. Some people are very skilled at twisting a set of facts around to make something that is actually false seem true. This is the danger of self-reliance, Swedenborg says: not only can we internally rationalize behavior that we know is wrong, but we can be more easily influenced by others.

According to Swedenborg, the serpent in Genesis 3 refers to our senses. Eve's senses told her that the apple looked delicious, and she wanted very much to eat it. She wanted to be like God—to determine her own course in life and to judge for herself what was right and wrong. That doesn't sound so bad, does it? But without a divine perspective, it's easy to misjudge a person or situation, or to act in a way that has unintentionally disastrous consequences.

Once Adam and Eve ate the fruit of the tree, their eyes were opened. They realized that they no longer had the innocent trust in God that they once did and that there was no going back. Before long, God knew it, too. He cursed the serpent to live on its belly and eat dust the rest of its life. That is what we do if we make evil part of our lives—casting our eyes down and turning away from God.

What God says next to the serpent you'll never see on a Christmas card, but Swedenborg tells us that it is the first prophecy in the Bible about God coming to earth in human form to overcome evil in the world: "And I will put hostility between you and the woman and between your seed and her seed. He will trample you on the head and you will wound him on the heel" (Genesis 3:15 [*Secrets of Heaven* §250]).

Eve, as the symbolic mother of everyone living, is described by Swedenborg as also a symbol of the first church on earth. As mentioned above, this is not a "church" as we think of it—a building, an organization—but the quality of faith and connection with God in individual hearts and minds. *Her seed* is the "church" that is to come, and the *he* who is to trample on the serpent's head is Jesus, who in Swedenborg's theology is the human incarnation of God.

It is interesting to note the parallels—no accident, to be sure—between Eve, who appears in the beginning of the Bible, and the woman clothed with the sun, who is mentioned in the book of Revelation. And the tree of life, which isn't mentioned again throughout the centuries of time covered by the Bible, suddenly is there again in Revelation—in the holy city descending from heaven.

Both women were symbols of the "church," the connection between God and the people throughout the Bible. Both women were set upon by serpents—which Swedenborg likens to the evil existing in all of us—who caused them pain in childbirth and threatened to devour their innocent offspring. The serpents do not prevail and evil is overcome, which is the hope and the promise for all of us: even when we have doubts about God, as individuals or as a culture, the people who want the spiritual sustenance of a connection with the Divine will always be able to find it.

The story of Adam and Eve reflects a pattern that we see play out throughout the Bible and sometimes in the history of the world: repeated trials, free choices and consequences, despair offset with hope, God's constant love, and—if we choose to receive it—his help in regaining our footing and continuing our regeneration.

In our spiritual journey, we are faced with the same choice as Eve. We can give in to the serpent and eat the apple; and we may do that at times, feeling that we know better and don't need God in our lives. Choosing that path has consequences, but there is always hope. When Adam and Eve were banished from the garden of Eden, that could have been the end. Swedenborg explains that because they had given in to the serpent, their intelligence and wisdom no longer were elevated and spiritual but were back down at ground level. And they—meaning all of us—had to learn real wisdom through hard work. We are not all cursed with the "original sin" of Adam and Eve, Swedenborg assures us, but we do have hereditary (today we might say genetic) inclinations toward evil and selfishness. We have our own battles to fight and our own gardens to grow. That is our personal path of regeneration.

The story of Adam and Eve also raises questions that many people still ponder: Why does God let it happen? Why did he allow Adam and Eve—and in turn the human race—to fall? Swedenborg explains that this was done to protect their freedom—and our freedom as well. We must be free to choose, even choosing against God; otherwise, we would not be truly human. And sometimes we must suffer the consequences of those actions in order to really understand why they were wrong. But God did not give up on the human race, then or now.

The story of Adam and Eve is also a morality tale for our lives. It started innocently, with the bite of an apple. And so it goes with our choices: we make little compromises, slight surrenders of integrity that may even feel good. Evil grows subtly and gradually, unless we do something about it. From the garden of Eden to the holy city described in the book of Revelation, the message and the challenge are the same: it always comes down to our choices.

Noah and the Ark

This is another familiar story mixed in with the fairy tales of our youth, and it has recently been rediscovered by Hollywood. Noah and his family load animals two by two into an ark, ride out a flood that covered the earth for forty days and forty nights, and survive to repopulate the earth. It's all very visual and powerful. The literal story has obvious lessons, but it strains credulity as a historical event. Could a flood really cover every living thing on earth and then recede? Where did all that water come from and where did it go? Would a loving God, in control of his universe, really destroy every person and animal he had created except for one family and a pair of each creature? What is this story really telling us?

Like the garden of Eden, Swedenborg asserts, it is an allegory, not a true story about people and events. But he also says that, as with everything else in the Bible, it is filled with spiritual truth, and everything it depicts is very real in our lives.

Swedenborg devotes hundreds of pages, primarily in *Secrets of Heaven,* to explaining the intricate spiritual sense of this story, greatly deepening its meaning and its relevance to our lives. On the surface, he says, it has to do with the fallen state of the church (the spiritual state of humanity) that existed before the Flood. But it is also about our own personal struggles, as we ride out a flood of temptations that come at us in waves and currents. The ark is the new church born within us—a new understanding and trust in God—that can carry us through hard times.

The story begins in Genesis 6:5: "And Jehovah saw that the evil of the people in the land multiplied; and everything that the thoughts of their heart fabricated was nothing but evil every day" (*Secrets of Heaven* §584).

The evil that multiplied was allowing their craving for material pleasures to overcome their understanding of what was good. Like Eve, they allowed themselves to be distracted by the promise of something shiny, convinced that they knew best what was right. So many people succumbed to this type of self-justification that the negative influences became overwhelming.

We can see this same dynamic at work in people's lives today. Some people chase money and power, others try to collect as many "toys" as they can, and others seek release in drugs and alcohol. The spiritual state described in the story of the Flood can be compared to people who struggle with addiction. In the beginning, the drugs, alcohol, or other substances feel good. The addicts tell themselves they can handle it—they're too smart to get hooked. Gradually, the substance abuse begins to take over their lives. When they "hit bottom," that's the Flood. They're so far gone that they can no longer find a way out on their own.

"But Noah found favor in Jehovah's eyes" (Genesis 6:8 [*Secrets of Heaven* §596]). Swedenborg teaches that whenever a church falls, there is always a remnant of good people who go on to build a new, truer faith. Noah represents that remnant. He is the means by which the human race can be saved from destruction, because God, in his love and mercy, wants more than anything else for human beings to survive and continue to grow.

Swedenborg goes on to say that this new church, this new state of religious being, was characterized by a love for humanity as a whole. It was the desire to do good for others because of that love, a desire that had almost been snuffed out by the sense-centered beliefs of the previous generation.

To go back to the example of addicts, Noah represents the bit of goodness and love that is still in them, despite anything they might do under the influence of a drug. Once rehabilitation begins and the controlling influence starts to recede, the love emerges again, like the sun from behind rain clouds. Now they can begin a new phase in their life.

In the Bible story, the ark represents the process of forming the new church. The birds and beasts and food that Noah is commanded to put into the ark all have corresponding meanings. Birds, as you may recall from the discussion of Creation, represent the logical reasoning of the intellect; animals represent a person's will, or driving impulses. Bringing food represents properly preparing the mind (the will and the intellect) for the changes to come. As Swedenborg puts it:

> The formation of the new church . . . is depicted by the ark that took in living things of every kind. But before that new church could come into being, it was necessary—as it always is—for the people in the church to suffer further trials, portrayed by the rising, tossing, and long ride of this ark on the flood waters. Their eventual transformation into truly spiritual people and their deliverance are depicted by the ebbing of the water. (*Secrets of Heaven* §605)

The voyage lasted for forty days and forty nights. What's the significance of that time period? Remember that Swedenborg says every number used in the Bible has a correspondence. The number forty represents adversity, a time of struggle and temptation before deliverance. Later in the Bible, Moses spends forty days and nights in anguish on Mount Sinai, without bread or water, before receiving the Ten Commandments. The children of Israel wandered the desert for forty years, complaining bitterly of their trials, before being delivered into Canaan—the Promised Land. Jesus submitted to being tempted by the devil for forty days and nights in the wilderness before his ultimate triumph.

Just as the story of Adam and Eve ends with a promise, so, too, does Noah's story end. After his family's deliverance, Noah builds an altar to give thanks and makes burnt offerings:

> And Jehovah smelled a restful smell, and Jehovah said in his heart, "I will never again curse the ground on the human being's account, because what human hearts fabricate is evil from their youth. And I will never again strike every living thing as I have done." (Genesis 8:21 [*Secrets of Heaven* §924])

This recognizes that we will always have evil with us. It is part of our heredity and our cultural environment, and it is there to test the freedom that defines us as human beings. But it also recognizes that God loves us despite this evil. God also said to Noah and his sons: "I am setting up my pact with you; and no more will all flesh be cut off by the waters of a flood, and no more will there be a flood to destroy the earth" (Genesis 9:11 [*Secrets of Heaven* §1031]).

This is an everlasting covenant, or promise, Swedenborg asserts—that no matter what trials we endure, God's love will always be with us and his church will never cease to exist somewhere on the earth. That is the ultimate triumph and hope of Noah and the Flood. Even when we feel as though we are flooded by our personal evils, even when we give up hope for ourselves, God doesn't give up hope for us.

This old story is not just another fable from long ago. It is a rich, spiritual story that relates to our lives right now. Swedenborg would tell searchers that they will never find the remains of the ark on Mount Ararat, because it never existed. That fact, he might add, should not dim our faith, because the real discovery is in the spiritual journey.

The Tower of Babel

Finally, we have the improbable story of the descendants of Noah setting out to build a city and a tower reaching into heaven. The ark was said to come to rest on Mount Ararat—a mountain three miles high. Could anyone possibly think that a tower of bricks could reach beyond that mountaintop into heaven? So what is this story really all about?

It is often interpreted as God's way of introducing mixed languages into the world as punishment. He confounds the people's plan to "reach into the heavens" by dispersing them with different tongues so they could no longer communicate. But as with everything else in the Bible, Swedenborg says, it is about much more—for example, our own inclination at times to turn away from God, as though we don't need him.

At the beginning of the story, "the whole earth had one language and the same words" (Genesis 11:1 [*Secrets of Heaven* §1284]). Swedenborg tells us that this *language* is actually spiritual understanding. You may remember that the church represented by Noah was one of mutual love. All of the people on earth at that time may have had different customs, but they had one goal, which was to love each other as they loved themselves.

This is the story, Swedenborg explains, of another judgment on a fallen church, or people, who had turned away from God because of their own greed. As such, it is a warning for all people who are prone to such self-absorbed delusions.

The descendants of Noah come to a plain in the land of Shinar and decide to settle there. They say to each other, "Come, let us make bricks and bake them until baked" (Genesis 11:3 [*Secrets of Heaven* §1294]). The verse goes on to say that they had brick for stone and that they had tar for mortar.

Why brick instead of the traditional stone used for building? Why tar instead of the usual clay mortar? Knowing the spiritual meaning, Swedenborg says, is the key to understanding the story.

Stones are made by God and stand for truth. Bricks are manufactured by us, like the kind of falsity we may come up with on our own and talk ourselves into believing. This represents putting ourselves ahead of God, or perverting doctrine to serve our own vision. Tar is a flammable substance, and burning the bricks represents the fire of self-love—the conceit that we know better and don't need to be told by God how to run our lives.

In the story, the people decide to build a tower so tall that it would reach up to the heavens. But God sees their intention and creates a confusion of languages so that they can't communicate, scattering them across the face of the earth.

Ironically, the zeal to build a tower reaching up to God really represents a downward spiral, Swedenborg explains. It is worshipping or believing in self rather than in God; it is focusing on gaining dominion over others. When charity—described as looking out for and serving one's neighbor—is gone from our lives, love of self and the world takes over. That is why in this story, God's "coming down" and scattering the people is really a judgment on this church.

They were scattered upon the face of the earth because they threatened to deprive others of the ability to know spiritual truth. They no longer had one common belief and goal but had a confusion of manufactured views—the incoherent babble of Babel—and therefore could no longer understand each other.

This is why, Swedenborg says, the state of this church had to be judged and changed. There was no longer any real worship of God in their hearts, minds, and lives. They were serving themselves.

So that strange tale of people setting out to build "a tower with its top in the heavens" (Genesis 11:4) is not just a story to engage our imagination but is something that still speaks to our own lives. We've all known what it's like to have feelings of selfishness and love of power, to turn away from God, and to delude ourselves that we can do just fine on our own.

We still see a lot of "tower-building" in the world, where people erect monuments of pride and self-gratification. But subordinating spiritual truth to human altars of brick and mortar will never extend our reach. Swedenborg explains that when our goal is the common good of society, God is with us. God cannot be present with people who care only about themselves.

Later in Genesis, Jacob, after he had stolen his father's blessing from his brother Esau and was tortured by guilt, traveled from Beersheba to Haran. He spent the night in a field, using a stone for a pillow. Here again is the image of a stone—Jacob's head was supported by truth. As he slept, he dreamed of a ladder reaching into heaven, with angels ascending and descending. When he awoke, he had a sudden realization of a new spirit in his life: "Surely the Lord is in this place," he said, "and I did not know it! . . . This is none other than the house of God, and this is the gate of heaven" (Genesis 28:16, 17).

Jacob used the stone to make an altar to thank God, and he vowed, "If God will be with me, and will keep me in this way that I go . . . so that I come again to my father's house in peace, then the Lord shall be my God, and this stone, which I have set up for a pillar, shall be God's house" (Genesis 28:20, 21–22).

This, Swedenborg tells us, is the consistent message and promise throughout the Bible, from the eleven allegorical chapters of Genesis through the Old and New Testaments to the end of Revelation: God is everywhere and always with us, even if it doesn't always seem apparent. With every choice we make, we are turning toward him or away from him—often without even being aware—but he never turns away from us. He is constantly with each of us, even when it may be the furthest thing from our minds: "Surely the Lord is in this place—and [we] did not know it." Anywhere and everywhere in our lives is a potential gateway to heaven—if we allow ourselves to be led there.

4

HIDDEN TREASURES: LOST AND FOUND

It is impossible to mentally or socially enslave a Bible-reading people. The principles of the Bible are the groundwork of human freedom.

— Horace Greeley

A thorough knowledge of the Bible is worth more than a college education.

— Theodore Roosevelt

For some years now I have read through the Bible twice every year. If you picture the Bible to be a mighty tree and every word a little branch, I have shaken every one of those branches because I wanted to know what it was and what it meant.

— Martin Luther

After those first eleven allegorical chapters of Genesis, the very next chapter plunges into the actual people, events, and history of the rest of the Bible. But it doesn't get any easier to understand.

Anyone's faith can be challenged by the many stories in the Old Testament that depict cruelty, violence, and injustice, which all seem so at odds with the image we might have of a just and loving God. Swedenborg explains, for instance, that women and babies aren't really being slaughtered in the destruction of Ai; rather, these passages deal with our love of worldly things and the consequences of that love. We may read about people turning to God and following him, then being lured away to worship idols instead. Those stories describe how we can feel devout and altruistic but also fall back on "false gods" any time we put our selfish and worldly desires ahead of God. Any story in which God seems to be acting angry or unjust actually illustrates our own spiritual journey—the trials and temptations, successes and setbacks—and will ultimately reassure us of God's constant presence with us.

Genesis 12 introduces Abram (later renamed Abraham) as a man chosen by God to be the patriarch of the children of Israel. God tells him to leave his country for a new land. "And I will make you into a great nation and bless you and make your name great, and you will be a blessing" (2 [*Secrets of Heaven* §1415]).

So Abram takes his beautiful wife Sarai (later renamed Sarah) through Canaan, and they are driven by famine into Egypt. One of the first things we see this great "man of God" do is ask his wife to tell the pharaoh that she is Abram's sister, not his wife. He wants her to lie so that "it may go well for me"—even though the pharaoh might then take her as his own wife (11–13 [*Secrets of Heaven* §§1465–77]).

In the mid-nineteenth century, a man who was struggling with the meaning of this very story was introduced, seemingly by chance, to the writings of Swedenborg and the revelation of the Bible's inner meaning while stranded on disease-plagued islands in the Caribbean. The man was John Bigelow (1817–1911), a prominent American journalist, lawyer, and statesman. Bigelow took on the corruption of Boss Tweed in New York City, was the US ambassador to France, befriended such prominent figures as German prince Otto von Bismarck, and helped to found the New York Public Library. As editor and co-owner of the *New York Evening Post,* he was fiercely anti-slavery at a time when this issue was one of the factors leading the country toward the Civil War. Bigelow had gone to Haiti in 1854 to see how this nation of former slaves was coping with self-government. There, he had a remarkable spiritual experience that would shape the rest of his life, one he would later describe in a book titled *The Bible That Was Lost and Is Found.*

While he was in Port-au-Prince for several weeks observing the natives, Haiti was, as he described it in his book, "desolated by yellow and other malignant fevers" (Bigelow 1953, 5). All but two of the crew who brought him there were already in the grave. It was hard to leave the island, but he managed to cross over to St. Thomas, hoping to find a ship sailing to New York. Then cholera broke out on St. Thomas, wiping out a tenth of the population within a month. With virtually no ships coming or going, Bigelow was stranded. The only other guest in his hotel was a Danish lawyer, identified in Bigelow's writings only as Mr. Kjerulff. They both read a lot. Bigelow was often immersed in his Bible.

In his book, Bigelow explains that his parents were strict Presbyterians. He had been sent off to boarding school at age eleven, where he became used to judging for himself "the logic and theological merits of what I heard from the pulpit and read in the Bible." He read with devotion but also with doubt and skepticism, and he "began quite early to discern what looked to me like inconsistencies and improbabilities in its pages" (8).

He always had questions and was searching for answers. How could there be mornings and evenings in the first days of Creation, he wondered, when the sun was not created until the fourth day? How could God allow suffering among his innocent offspring? How could Christ's death be "the ultimate sacrifice" if Christ knew he would rise three days after his crucifixion? The more Bigelow read, the more questions he had.

"This taste for hunting and running down what seemed to me incongruous, inconsistent or inconsequential passages of the letter of the Word," he wrote, "grew by what it fed on, and it is mortifying and painful for me now to think how blind and stupid I was all this time" (10). Bigelow still found the Bible to be the most interesting book in his library but had come to feel that it held no higher meaning to him than did the writings of Marcus Aurelius or Confucius. Its stories attracted and mystified him.

One night in St. Thomas, he was reading Genesis 12 in the hotel dining room when he commented to Kjerulff: "Is it not extraordinary that this book should be accepted by the most highly civilized nations of the earth as the Word of God? Just listen." Then Bigelow read the verses about Abram, who was "selected from all the people of the earth as most deserving of [God's] favour" but who told his wife to lie for him. "Does not the Egyptian [the pharaoh]," he asked, "whom the Bible represents as the oppressor of God's people, appear . . . to have been the better man of the two?" (14).

Kjerulff quietly agreed that it appeared so, but asked him if he had ever read Emanuel Swedenborg. Kjerulff briefly explained Swedenborg's *Secrets of Heaven,* a work that spanned eight volumes in the original Latin and revealed word by word and phrase by phrase the internal, spiritual meaning of the books of Genesis and Exodus.

Bigelow had never heard of Swedenborg, but was immediately struck by the opening passages in *Secrets of Heaven:*

> The Word in the Old Testament contains secrets of heaven, and every single aspect of it has to do with the Lord, his heaven, the church, faith, and all the tenets of faith; but not a single person

sees this in the letter. In the letter, or literal meaning, people see only that it deals for the most part with the external facts of the Jewish religion.

The truth is, however, that every part of the Old Testament holds an inner message. Except at a very few points, those inner depths never show on the surface. The exceptions are concepts that the Lord revealed and explained to the apostles, such as the fact that the sacrifices symbolize the Lord, and that the land of Canaan and Jerusalem symbolize heaven (which is why it is called the heavenly Canaan or Jerusalem [Galatians 4:26; Hebrews 11:16 and 12:22; Revelation 21:2, 10]), as does Paradise.

The Christian world, though, remains deeply ignorant of the fact that each and every detail down to the smallest—even down to the tiniest jot—enfolds and symbolizes spiritual and heavenly matters; and because it lacks such knowledge, it also lacks much interest in the Old Testament.

Still, Christians can come to a proper understanding if they reflect on a single notion: that since the Word is the Lord's and comes from him, it could not possibly exist unless it held within it the kinds of things that have to do with heaven, the church, and faith. Otherwise it could not be called the Lord's Word, nor could it be said to contain any life. Where, after all, does life come from if not from what is living? That is, if not from the fact that every single thing in the Word relates to the Lord, who is truly life itself? Whatever does not look to him at some deeper level, then, is without life; in fact, if a single expression in the Word does not embody or reflect him in its own way, it is not divine.

Without this interior life, the Word in its letter is dead. It resembles a human being, in that a human has an outward self and an inward one, as the Christian world knows. The outer being, separated from the inner, is just a body and so is dead, but the inward being is what lives and allows the outward being to live. The inner being is a person's soul.

In the same way, the letter of the Word by itself is a body without a soul. (§§1–3)

Swedenborg goes on to state that "without the Lord's aid not a soul can possibly see that this is the case" (§5).

Well, that got Bigelow's attention. Finally, someone was telling him that his questions might be answered. He was skeptical but hopeful.

When he got to the section that was troubling him in Genesis 12, he was told by Swedenborg: "True history begins here." But, Swedenborg added, it is also important to know that "all the elements are representative, and the individual words are symbolic" (*Secrets of Heaven* §1401).

How could a text be "true history" and at the same time be representative and symbolic? Swedenborg says that these stories describe people who actually lived and events that really happened, but the pattern of these people's lives was shaped in such a way that the stories would also carry a much deeper meaning. To put it another way, by reading these histories, a person who understands their inner meaning is reminded of the spiritual principles involved. The literal meaning serves as a pointer or shorthand reference to the deeper meaning of the story—to the point where a person well versed in correspondences isn't reading the details of the story at all but directly understands the spiritual significance of what's being described.

That all the facts of biblical history are representative and the words symbolic, Swedenborg says,

> is true of all the narrative parts of the Word —not only the books of Moses but Joshua, Judges, Samuel, and Kings as well. Nothing but history appears in any of them. Yet although the literal meaning is a history, the inner meaning holds the mysteries of heaven, which lie hidden there. These mysteries can never be seen, as long as we train our mind's eye on the historical details; they are not unveiled until we withdraw our minds from the literal meaning. (*Secrets of Heaven* §1408)

As with many readers of the Old Testament, Bigelow had trouble trying to reconcile the violence and cruelty that seemed to be condoned and even encouraged by God with his desire to see the Divine as pure love and mercy. He was much relieved to read in

Swedenborg's explanation of the literal sense that its features are "like facts that we glean from our sense impressions and retain in our memory. These are general containers that hold deeper levels inside. . . . The containers are earthly; their vital contents are spiritual and heavenly." So throughout the historical context of the Bible, Swedenborg says, what is spiritual and heavenly is always within these earthly containers, but they "never enter our field of vision except through the inner meaning" (*Secrets of Heaven* §1408:2).

Bigelow wrote that he was intrigued but still cautious, "expecting to drop the book as soon as I came to something—and I did not in the least doubt I soon should—that would be so absurd, or improbable, or illogical, as would justify me, without rudeness, in returning the book to my Danish friend with thanks."

But, he confesses, "though I understood but imperfectly what I read, I did not find what I was looking for; I found nothing that I could point to with confidence and say, 'There, you see your man Swedenborg must have been either a fool or an impostor, if not both.' On the other hand, I did find several curious and striking things which piqued my curiosity. For example, his opening comments on the first verse of the chapter showed me that at least I was following a thoughtful guide. I had neither heard nor read anything like it before" (Bigelow 1953, 19).

The opening verse of Genesis 12 says, "And Jehovah said to Abram, 'Go your way from your land and from your birth[place] and from your father's house to the land that I show you'" (*Secrets of Heaven* §1407).

Swedenborg explains that in the inner sense, *Abram* symbolizes God, and he also represents the spiritual potential within each of us. *Jehovah said to Abram* symbolizes the dawning realization when we hear something that contains a deep spiritual truth. *Go your way from your land and from your birth[place]* means withdrawing from the superficial pleasures of the world. *And from your father's house* speaks about the deeper levels of our earthly existence—the ones that touch on the things we have learned, our emotional reactions, and our attachments. We must also withdraw from these things, Swedenborg tells us, if we want to journey *to the land that I show you,* that is, to an understanding of higher spiritual wisdom. This first verse, then, is setting the stage for the rest of the story.

In Genesis 12, we have the story about Abram and Sarai, newcomers in Egypt. Because Abram fears that the Egyptians will take his beautiful wife for themselves and kill him, he asks Sarai to lie and say that she is his sister. The ruse works at first; Sarai is taken to the pharaoh's house, and Abram is given livestock and valuables. But Jehovah sends plagues upon the pharaoh's house, whereupon the pharaoh discovers the deception and sends Sarai back to Abram.

The inner meaning, according to Swedenborg, is quite different. Even though Jesus would not be born for thousands of years, the spiritual meaning within the Bible is never bound by time and space. So, Swedenborg explains, this story of Abram is actually about the life of Jesus from childhood to adolescence, when he was seeking knowledge (represented by Abram's going to Egypt). Jesus set out with a collection of earthly facts, but he had no understanding of how to marry them to deeper spiritual truth—in terms of the sequence of the story, Abram was not yet mature enough to present Sarai as his wife in front of the Egyptians. All Jesus had was an intuitive sense that there was a deeper knowledge to be gained, and that intuitive sense is represented by Sarai as Abram's sister. The pharaoh represents the study of religious knowledge; in Jesus's case, his quest for truth led him to seek a better understanding of religious practice, and for a while, that worked very well. But there comes a time in our spiritual growth when the facts we've learned have taken us as far as they can; and when that time comes, we must forget everything we've learned and embrace a higher truth. The shedding of old knowledge is represented in this story by the plagues sent to the pharaoh. The end result is a realization that we must listen to the voice of divine truth within us; the facts we've learned must be used to support our love and trust in God, not to support our egotistical thoughts and emotions. Only when Jesus reaches this state of openness can his outer mind be wedded to his inner spiritual self: Abram is reunited with Sarai as his wife.

Swedenborg sums up the story this way:

> Anyone who pays attention can see that in itself a store of religious knowledge is just a means for becoming rational, then spiritual, and at last heavenly. The knowledge can then bring our outer being into contact with our inner being, and when this happens, our study of it has served its true purpose. (*Secrets of Heaven* §1472:2)

So while Swedenborg interprets Abram and Sarai's story in terms of Jesus's spiritual journey, he also describes Jesus's spiritual development as a template for our own mental and spiritual growth as human beings.

Intrigued by this interpretation, Bigelow spent a day searching out other stories that had troubled him: the frauds perpetrated by Abram and Isaac; Jacob and his mother Rebekah conspiring to cheat Esau out of his blessing; Jacob enriching himself at the expense of his uncle Laban; and Rachel stealing her father's sacred images, then lying to him about it.

The story of Jacob—the stealing of his brother Esau's blessing; the treachery of both his mother, Rebekah, and his wife Rachel, then being fearfully reunited with Esau—is fraught with drama and spiritual meaning. It is filled with apparent deceit and injustice, both of which are only explained in the spiritual meaning.

In the first part of the story, Jacob and his twin brother Esau are depicted as two very different people. Esau, described as red and hairy, is a hunter and a "man of the field," and he is loved by their father, Isaac. Jacob is described as a "quiet man, living in tents" (Genesis 25:27). One day, when Isaac is old and nearly blind, he calls Esau and asks him to go out and hunt, to prepare food from what he captures, and to bring that food to Isaac so that Isaac may bless him. Rebekah, hearing this, tells Jacob instead to go out and kill two young goats for her to cook. She helps him disguise himself as Esau and take the food to Isaac, who is fooled into giving

Jacob the blessing. When Esau returns, he is furious to discover the deception, but Isaac cannot take back Jacob's blessing, so he instead gives Esau a blessing of a different sort, promising that while Esau would serve Jacob, one day he would break free from Jacob's rule.

What are we to make of this deception? Swedenborg explains that this story is really about the spiritual principles of good and truth and about the process of regeneration by which a person is spiritually reborn. Jacob represents spiritual truths and doctrines that we have learned during the course of our life. Esau represents goodness, but it is an earthly goodness and so one motivated by selfish emotions and a love of physical pleasures.

In this story, Isaac's old age represents the passage from one stage of spiritual being into another. Swedenborg tells us that there comes a point in the process of regeneration when truth must come to the fore: we must put aside our selfish instincts and start to live according to the moral teachings we have learned, even if such behavior doesn't come naturally to us. But our will—the part of our mind that drives our actions—resists being guided by truth. The will loves those worldly pleasures, and it won't give them up easily. Thus the rational mind, represented here by Rebekah, must step in and help show the will the way by bringing to our attention truths just as our conscience reminds us to act morally when our emotions guide us elsewhere. When Isaac learns of the deception, he is described as "trembl[ing] violently" (Genesis 27:33), a physical reaction to the difficult mental and spiritual process of letting go of his former desires. Esau's angry reaction describes how our ego responds to being denied something that it wants: a temper tantrum. And yet, Swedenborg tells us, eventually a person's will must be reformed; as we travel along the path of spiritual growth and regeneration, we will over time desire to do good out of spiritual rather than selfish motivations. When that day comes, the rules we have learned once again take a back seat: Esau will in time break free from Jacob's dominion and become the ruler.

In the story, Jacob fears Esau's wrath and flees to his uncle Laban, with whom he spends many years. He first marries Laban's daughter Leah and then her sister Rachel, having children with both women. It is only after twenty years of hard work, representative of spiritual progress, that Jacob is ready to return home to face his brother.

On the journey home, Jacob spends all night in the wilderness, where a "man wrestled with him until daybreak" (Genesis 32:24), dislocating Jacob's hip. We don't know from the telling if the man is God, an angel, or his own conscience. Swedenborg tells us, though, that the act of wrestling represents a time of inner turmoil, a conflict between Jacob—representing a love of truth—and the temptation to reject or misuse that truth for personal gain. Ultimately, Jacob wins the battle and comes into a greater state of spiritual understanding. Then he is blessed and given a new name, Israel, signifying that he will head a great nation.

But in a person who is regenerating, truth can never take priority over a love of goodness. When Jacob and his family first encounter Esau, Esau has brought an army of four hundred men with him. Seeing this, Jacob is afraid and bows down before Esau. But Esau runs to meet him, and they embrace. Swedenborg tells us that Esau now represents divine good, the drive to do good things in the world out of a love and compassion that come from God. Esau running to meet Jacob is the image of divine love flowing into us, a transformative experience that is not possible until we humble ourselves and admit that the truths we've learned aren't enough to carry us forward.

Swedenborg says that the story of Jacob and the trials that he and his family endured is also our story, the story of spiritual rebirth. In the chapter on the Creation, we saw a broad overview of how the process of regeneration works. Here, with Jacob, we examine one short stretch of that road in much greater detail. And all along our journey, we see the same message over and over again: we may turn away from God at times, pursuing our own ends, but he is never distant or removed. God is always with us, even if we do not know it.

And if we "wrestle" our way through regeneration, we can be elevated just as Jacob was.

These are just the opening chapters of the Bible, with centuries of strife and drama still to come. It all illustrates our own journey, Swedenborg says—something that goes on throughout our lives, influenced by the daily choices we make. The Bible is not only a guidebook for our lives on earth but also for the eternal lives of our spirit.

John Bigelow found Swedenborg as if by chance, after years of puzzling over the Bible's mysteries. His experience was not the same as Paul's epiphany on the road to Damascus but was rather a process fueled by doubt and discovery. Once introduced to Swedenborg's teachings, though, he said he felt like a blind man who suddenly could see. His studies convinced him that the answers he sought—which have also baffled the faithful and the skeptics for centuries—lay in a deeper interpretation of the literal words of the Bible.

5

EXODUS: IT'S YOUR JOURNEY, TOO

Though in a wilderness, man is never alone.
— Sir Thomas Browne

When you have read the Bible, you will know it is the word of
God, because you will have found it the key to your heart, your
own happiness, and your own duty.
— Woodrow Wilson

The Bible holds up before us ideals that are within sight of
the weakest and the lowliest, and yet so high that the best and
noblest are kept with their faces turned ever upward. It carries
the call of the Savior to the remotest corners of the earth; on its
pages are written the assurances of the present and our hopes for
the future.
— William Jennings Bryan

The book of Genesis is epic in itself: from the creation of the world and the garden of Eden to the fall of humankind with Noah and the Flood; from the sons of Jacob selling their favored brother Joseph into slavery in Egypt, to him rising to power there and eventually being reconciled with his brothers, to his family themselves becoming slaves in Egypt. But beyond Genesis, the Old Testament is filled with much more: stirring drama, ancient laws, an angry God "smiting" armies and innocents, the soothing poetry of the Psalms, inspiring heroes, and troubling tragedies.

Among the better-known stories of the Old Testament are David and Goliath, Samson and Delilah, Jonah and the whale, and Daniel in the lions' den. But before all that is the drama of Moses and the children of Israel, who flee slavery in Egypt and wander forty years in the wilderness before being led into the Promised Land. Swedenborg tells us that every detail in each of these stories—no matter how obscure or seemingly irrelevant—speaks to our lives. He describes the Bible as a reflection of our own trials and temptations, our choices and challenges. We saw varying aspects of the journey to growth and regeneration reflected in different stories from Genesis; but now, in the book of Exodus, the full story is laid out.

The story resonates across cultures and centuries. Exodus has special significance for the Jewish people because it is the story of their own history and deliverance. But it is important to everyone, Swedenborg says, because it is really the story of our own journey out of any slavery in our lives and into our own promised land.

Exodus means to leave. In the literal sense, the story describes the children of Israel leaving their captivity in Egypt; in the spiritual sense, it refers to all of us leaving old ways behind in a journey to change our life.

That story begins with Moses, the child of an Israelite couple living in Egypt. Afraid of the growing influence of the Israelite community, the pharaoh has ordered that all male Israelite infants be killed. To save Moses's life, his parents leave him in a basket that is set adrift on the Nile. He is rescued by a daughter of the pharaoh and becomes her son. One of the first stories we are told about Moses as an adult is a strange one: "He saw an Egyptian beating a Hebrew, one of his kinsfolk," as it is recorded in the Bible; he quickly looked around and, when he saw that no one was watching, "he killed the Egyptian and hid him in the sand." Then he was afraid of being found out and "fled from Pharaoh [and] settled in the land of Midian" (Exodus 2:11, 12, 15).

What does this ancient act mean for us? Swedenborg tells us that Egypt, and by extension the people of Egypt, represent facts we learn. The Hebrew in this story represents the truth. What is actually portrayed here is an internal process: Moses recognizes that the facts he's learned are overwhelming the spiritual truth he's only just started to sense. He responds by killing the Egyptian and hiding his body in the sand—banishing those facts from his mind and focusing on inner truth. But in order to truly deepen his understanding, he has to separate himself from the world and focus on study, symbolized by his retreat to Midian. This is the beginning of Moses's journey, and it is also the beginning of our own spiritual journey: recognizing that there is more to life than it seems but that achieving deeper meaning requires hard work.

While in Midian, as the story goes, an angel of the Lord appears to Moses on Mount Horeb, in a bush that was burning but not consumed by the fire. God called to Moses from the midst of the bush and told him to take off his sandals, "for the place on which you are standing is holy ground" (Exodus 3:5). God went on to say that he had seen the suffering of the Israelites in Egypt and had come to deliver them into a new land "flowing with milk and honey" (Exodus 3:8). He was calling on Moses to lead them, but Moses wasn't ready for this. Moses didn't feel prepared to lead anyone. "Who am I," he asked, "that I should go to Pharaoh, and bring the Israelites out of Egypt?" But God assured him, "I will be with you" (Exodus 3:11, 12).

The spiritual meaning for us, Swedenborg says, is that taking off our shoes is a way of raising our focus from earthly distractions so that we can really hear God's voice. It's like turning off the TV, getting away from e-mail and Facebook, and escaping all the demands on our attention so that we can sit quietly and contemplate a garden or a sunset—so we can just listen. That is how we "draw near" to God, he says. It is something we cannot do physically but can do with our spirit.

Swedenborg teaches that we all are living spiritual as well as earthly lives in this world, although we are not conscious of it. And because our spiritual lives are what will continue eternally, making our natural lives just a blink of an eye by comparison, we should be feeding our spirits as regularly and purposefully as we do our natural bodies.

We can feel alive and energized in this life, he says, while also being spiritually asleep—and therefore stuck—without even realizing it. He likens this to the story in the Gospels about the disciples who were sleeping while Jesus was praying in Gethsemane, the night before the soldiers came to arrest him. When Jesus finds the disciples asleep after having asked them to remain awake with him, he chastises Peter: "So, could you not stay awake with me one hour?" Then he says to them, and says to us: "Stay awake and pray that you may not come into the time of trial; the spirit indeed is willing, but the flesh is weak" (Matthew 26:40–41). Even after this warning, however, he left them twice more to pray and each time again found them asleep. Does he also find us asleep when we should be "staying awake and praying"?

When we are spiritually unaware amid all that is going on around us, Swedenborg warns, we should be listening for God's voice. Just as God called Moses and the children of Israel out of Egypt, he calls us to leave whatever we are slaves to and follow him.

Sometimes we have to shut out all the noise and really listen. "There was a great wind . . . but the Lord was not in the wind; and after the wind an earthquake, but the Lord was not in the earthquake; and after the earthquake a fire, but the Lord was not in the fire; and after the fire a sound of sheer silence" (1 Kings 19:11–12).

"Be still, and know that I am God" (Psalm 46:10).

The time to be still and listen for that "sound of sheer silence," Swedenborg tells us, is when we are reading the Bible and trying to understand what God is saying to us. What is the message from so long ago that applies to us right now?

Once we become spiritually awake, he adds, and confront what we need to be released from, we are ready for the journey. This is the next step in the process—we realize that we need the silence in order to embrace the truth; and once we understand our direction, all we have to do is listen to the guidance of that inner voice. God assures us that we will always be free to make choices, such as whether to let go of whatever it is that enslaves us. It takes courage, and it won't be an easy trip, but, he promises, "I will be with you."

The poet Elizabeth Barrett Browning was a devoted reader of Swedenborg, so there is special significance in these lines from the seventh chapter of her epic, religiously themed poem *Aurora Leigh:*

> Earth's crammed with heaven,
> And every common bush afire with God;
> But only he who sees, takes off his shoes,
> The rest sit round it, and pluck blackberries. (Browning 1917, 86)

She is challenging us, as Moses was challenged. Do we see the fire, take off our shoes, and answer the call—or are we distracted by the momentary pleasure of picking blackberries?

Swedenborg says that experiencing Egypt in our lives is also a time of preparation. We train ourselves for careers, prepare for marriage, and plan for retirement. A medical student may feel overwhelmed while trying to master all there is to learn, but he or she will later become a skilled and confident doctor. In the same way, we can train ourselves for our spiritual journey, although it takes work and sacrifice as well. But, he suggests, we all can feel something of the mountaintop moment Moses experienced. We can hear God speak from a flame of fire anytime we sense spiritual enlightenment or inspiration— that sound of sheer silence within us.

Moses was afraid of confronting the pharaoh, as we may shrink from confronting whatever controls us. He thought the pharaoh would kill him. And Swedenborg says that something actually may need to die inside us to get us moving forward. In this story, that something is represented by the ten horrible plagues that God sent to the Egyptians. Swedenborg tells us that the inner meaning of each of these plagues —water turning to blood; frogs; gnats; flies; diseased livestock; boils; thunder and hail; locusts; darkness; and finally the death of the Egyptians' firstborn children—represents a different type of evil or false idea living inside us. The successive waves of plagues illustrate a process Swedenborg calls *devastation*, in which the negative feelings and desires inside us are gradually replaced by good ones, enabling us to rise above our lower earthly nature. For someone going through this process, it may feel like death, but if successful, it will lead to greater freedom. In the context of this story, in order to be free, the worldly things represented by Egypt had to die.

Swedenborg explains that the "pharaoh" who rules in us is like the constant effort made by spirits in hell to turn us away from God so that we will indulge in selfish loves. But God is just as constantly fighting these battles with and for us, as shown in Exodus, where God guides Moses and Aaron at every step along the way.

The children of Israel represent our own spiritual potential. We don't feel like slaves—at least not like the children of Israel, who were forced to make bricks for the cities of the Egyptians. But just as they felt stuck in their captivity and unable to escape, we can become slaves to our own habits, behaviors, or compulsions. Smokers, for instance, may live with the illusion that they can quit whenever they want—until they try to stop. Then they may find they are stuck, that their addiction is a form of slavery, and that freeing themselves involves a lot of trial and testing.

We may find ourselves stuck in Egypt at times, just as they did. The danger is that we might actually enjoy it at first and not recognize the silky bonds of slavery. We may be so caught up in selfish pleasures that we lose sight of Canaan. This is when the power of the hells can be most subtle and insidious. We may feel good about what we are doing when in actuality we are slipping away from where we want to be.

It is easy to be content with the pleasures and comforts of the world—our iPads and flat-screen TVs, nice restaurants, and Caribbean cruises. Heavenly goals may seem out of reach among the demands of this world. Swedenborg says that Moses wants us to fight for what we believe in, while the pharaoh instills fear. The pharaoh is the voice inside us telling us not to fight back but to give up.

Even though the children of Israel desperately wanted to get out of Egypt, a lot of bargaining went on, just as we may bargain between our instincts and our conscience. "Wait a minute," we might say. "We don't have to be quite so drastic. Let's wait for a better day." Any time we set out to change our lives, there is apt to be conflict in our minds. This is represented by the children of Israel experiencing the plagues and death in Egypt, with the pharaoh making promises and then going back on them. The children of Israel had to deal with these trials before they could summon the courage to escape.

Courage did not come easily to the children of Israel, and it doesn't come easily to us when we face adversity. They saw the calamities in Egypt and the mercurial temperament of the pharaoh, and they figured they might be better off just staying and serving the Egyptians than risking their lives in the wilderness.

Imagine their exhilaration when they finally escaped, six hundred thousand strong, after hundreds of years of captivity. They had the dream of a promised land and a sense of purpose. But they were also filled with anxiety. They probably thought it would be an easy journey once they got away. Perhaps it would take them a month or so. If they had known all that was to come—for another forty years!—they probably would have given up hope and stayed in Egypt. Indeed, they were ready to turn back when they met their first obstacle.

When they came to the Red Sea, that was daunting enough. While they despaired over what to do, the pharaoh had another change of heart and sent his army after them. So there they were, between the devil and the Red Sea. They turned bitterly on Moses, complaining that they would have been better off stuck in slavery than slaughtered in the wilderness.

Moses gave them an important message that should resonate anytime we face a crisis: Stand still. Listen for the voice of God. Then go forward, with the Lord leading.

That is not our instinct, and it certainly wasn't what the children of Israel wanted to hear. Standing still did not make sense. Neither did going forward. In such times of crisis, it is easy to lose faith and even be angry with God for encouraging us on the journey and then seeming to abandon us when the going gets rough. God knows we will have ups and downs in our lives—our careers, families and marriages, and anything we pursue with passion. He knows we will sometimes despair over challenges that seem overwhelming. But, Swedenborg teaches, he sees what we cannot. He knows how to get us through "the sea of troubles" if we will but obey his word, trust in him, and follow.

The Red Sea was an impossible barrier, but the people were told to go forward, to walk toward it. That required a leap of faith. And that is when God gave them the miracle of Moses parting the sea so they could cross safely, and then God let the water rush back in to drown the pursuing Egyptians.

We may feel we have been there, facing all that hell can throw at us to discourage our journey, which is what the Red Sea represents. Winston Churchill once echoed what the children of Israel were told: "If you're going through hell, keep going." It takes trust in something greater than ourselves to overcome "impossible" road blocks. Swedenborg tells us that the parting of the Red Sea represents the power of God to defeat all obstacles; the trust the Israelites showed in stepping through those walls of water represents the faith we need to have in order to progress to the next step. Everyone who tries to overcome some internal compulsion eventually reaches a point where they realize they can't do it on their own, and they need to trust in a higher power.

As Swedenborg puts it: "During our spiritual tests, we are apparently left completely alone, although in fact we are not alone—at those times God is most intimately present at our deepest level giving us support" (*True Christianity* §126).

Once delivered from the Egyptians, the children of Israel must have felt the worst was over and that God and Moses really had saved them. But there were more trials ahead, just as we find in our lives.

After escaping from the Red Sea, they wandered for three days with nothing to drink. They must have been thinking: "This is the Promised Land? It seems more like a wasteland." So imagine how relieved they must have been to come upon the water of Marah, how they rushed toward it—and then how devastated they must have felt to find the water so foul they couldn't drink it. Of course they complained bitterly to Moses. He was as crushed as they were, and he cried out to God for help.

God showed Moses a piece of wood, and Moses "threw it into the water, and the water became sweet" (Exodus 15:25). This is another illustration of the spiritual sense within the Bible. The water in this story represents spiritual truth. It is too bitter to drink because the truths have begun to fail them: the Israelites thought that the road would be easy, and then they realized just how challenging it would be. They were thinking back to the comforts of Egypt and wondering why they left. Facing our own weakness can be like that. We might think after a personal breakthrough that we've conquered all obstacles and that the road ahead will be smooth, and then we run into setbacks. Our old cravings start to kick in. Our ego takes over. The spiritual truths that have brought us some freedom suddenly seem unpalatable.

At that point in the story, God had Moses throw that branch into the bitter water, which made it sweet. Swedenborg says that's because wood symbolizes goodness from God that can transform us. In this case, God reminded the Israelites—and the story reminds us—of the good that can come from spiritual growth, even during difficult times. That's when we thirst for guiding truth in our lives—the sweet water that God offers.

Turning a bitter experience into something good and lasting in our lives, Swedenborg says, is an illustration of the way God leads us, just as he led the children of Israel in the wilderness. Acknowledging the lessons and the good that come out of an experience gives us perspective on why we need to face temptation and trials to make progress in our spiritual journeys.

Chuck Colson, a man who transformed his reputation from infamy to integrity during Washington's tumultuous Watergate era, is an example of a life transformed by sweet water. Colson began his career in American politics with enviable accomplishment, but he ended it with shame and imprisonment. Then, with God's help, he found a life of significance.

As a young man, he was an ambitious lawyer in Washington, DC, and he became the top legal counsel for President Richard Nixon. He described himself as a ruthlessly loyal hatchet man. His actions led to him being charged with obstruction of justice when the Nixon administration attempted to cover up its involvement in a break-in at the Democratic National Committee headquarters in the Watergate office complex. Colson went to prison, but he came out a changed man, often quoting Russian martyr Aleksandr Solzhenitsyn: "Bless you, prison, for having been in my life!" (Solzhenitsyn 1974, 617)

Colson had a religious conversion before he went to prison. He began working with prisoners and devoted the rest of his life to them until he died at age eighty in 2012. He founded Prison Fellowship Ministries to help prisoners and their families. He mobilized thousands of volunteers to give them hope, established programs to help them find jobs, and made society a little better. The bitter water he had been drinking became sweet once goodness and purpose—serving "the least of our brethren"—replaced the selfish obsessions that had driven his life.

Here was a man who was on top of the world in the White House and came to realize he'd been stuck in Egypt. In helping to turn predatory criminals into productive citizens, he found goodness and satisfaction in the sweet water of serving God and his neighbor.

We don't have to experience the extremes of Chuck Colson's life—or the Israelites' forty years in the wilderness—to realize that we always need to be replenished with the sweet water of core truths and goodness in our lives.

By the second month of the Israelites' journey, food supplies were running out and they began complaining again. They accused Moses of bringing them into the wilderness to die. Their bodies—and their souls—were starving.

But God knows our needs before we do, Swedenborg notes, and provides what we need. God gave them bread every morning, but he gave just what they needed to sustain them. Since the people didn't know what this strange substance on the ground was, they asked, "What is it?" The Hebrew word they used was *manna*. Moses answered them, "It is the bread that the Lord has given you to eat" (Exodus 16:15). In the spiritual sense, Swedenborg says, manna represents goodness and blessings that we receive from God, and it could also be said to represent God himself coming into our lives and watching over us.

The people were told to gather just as much manna as their families needed each day, nothing more. That's a lesson for us as well: to be satisfied with what we have and not be greedy. By asking the people not to gather more than they needed, Moses was asking them to trust that God would provide enough to sustain them.

Manna was more than just what the people needed to keep from starving. "Bread from heaven" (Exodus 16:4) is given to nourish our spirit as well. This is the joy we find in life: the delight in helping others and the feelings of hope and peace. Here again, we need to trust that we receive as much as we have the ability to absorb.

We know what changing our diet can mean for our earthly bodies. The children of Israel missed "the fleshpots of Egypt"—their selfish pleasures. They had to change their diet to heavenly food, to look beyond their own needs and think of others.

Working to become a better person, however, is a lifetime process, with plenty of pitfalls along the way. Just when we feel good about our progress, we may slide backward. When all is going well, we would never think of hurting a friend. But at the end of a long, frustrating day, when we're a little cranky and worn down, a cutting, hurtful remark may spill out. Hell doesn't attack us when we're in a good place emotionally and spiritually, Swedenborg says, but when we're tired and vulnerable. Battles along the way may seem to come out of the blue.

That's what happened to the children of Israel. After escaping the Egyptians and getting the food and water they needed, their journey still loomed endlessly, but at least they seemed safe. Then, just as they approached Mount Sinai, they were attacked by Amalek and his army.

They were simple travelers, not looking for trouble, and they certainly were not prepared for soldiers. But they were suddenly under attack, and Moses called on Joshua to choose men to fight the Amalekites.

Swedenborg says that wars in the Bible always represent the struggle between good and evil within our own minds. We can find ourselves set upon by Amalekites when we least expect it. "These hellish demons never attack us openly," Swedenborg writes, "and never when our resistance is high, only when it looks as though we are slipping and about to succumb. Then suddenly they are there to give us a final push" (*Secrets of Heaven* §8593:2).

The children of Israel were vulnerable and under an attack they hadn't foreseen. We aren't told how the battle between Joshua's forces and Amalek's army played out except through the curious role of Moses. When he held his arms up—in the same way that he lifted his arms when parting the Red Sea—the children of Israel prevailed. When his arms tired and drooped, the Amalekites gained the upper hand. When Moses called for help, Aaron and Hur helped hold up his arms, and the Amalekites were defeated.

Swedenborg says that Moses knew he needed help, just as we need help in our battles. Aaron was a priest and Hur was a layman. The message, Swedenborg explains, is that when we face battles, we need to lift up our arms to God as a sign of faith and trust, as Moses did. Just as the children of Israel found themselves suddenly under attack, we may be called to fight or stand up for what is true and right, sometimes when we least expect it. When Moses looks upward and raises his arms, he is looking to God for support; when he lowers his arms, he is looking to himself and the world for strength. As Swedenborg puts it:

> When faith looked toward the Lord, truth engaged in battle won, and when it looked down, away from the Lord toward self-aggrandizement and materialism, falsity won, as symbolized by Israel's prevailing when Moses raised his hand and Amalek's prevailing when he lowered it. (*Secrets of Heaven* §8604:4)

When we look to God, Swedenborg says, we never fight alone—unless we think we can win without him. This story of Moses and the Amalekites is telling us to face our challenges openly and constructively and to let God give us the patience, trust, and confidence to prevail.

As dramatic as the Israelites' journey had been in its early stages, the most significant experience of those forty years occurred in the third month, as the children of Israel approached Mount Sinai.

The pillars of cloud and fire that had been guiding them led them to this place and stopped before the mountain. Imagine the mix of fear and wonder of the children of Israel on the third day when the mountain was covered with a thick cloud, filled with lightning and thunder. Then came the sound of a summoning trumpet, and the people nervously advanced to the foot of the mountain.

God descended and spoke the words that today are the core expression of Christian morality, a set of values shared by many cultures and faiths: the Ten Commandments, hewn on two tablets brought down by Moses.

This was the milestone on the journey. Until then, they were just a group of travelers, looking for a land "flowing with milk and honey" (Exodus 3:8). Now their journey and their lives were transformed. Now they knew what they would live by. Now they were choosing to follow God.

Up to this point, God led them through miracles, outward signs that compelled their belief. Now they were getting to know God in a new way. Now he was guiding them as he guides us, when what is written on stone becomes etched in our hearts.

But even the dramatic process of giving the people the Ten Commandments (Exodus 20:2–17) was not enough to convince the children of Israel to change their ways. Picture the ominous setting. As Moses ascends the mountain, not to be seen again for forty days and forty nights, it is covered with a thick cloud full of lightning and thunder. The fearful people promise to be obedient. But without Moses to keep them focused, they turn to Aaron and plead with him to make them a golden calf, an idol that the people could appeal to for protection after Moses appears to have abandoned them. On a literal level, this shows how easy it was for them to break the commandment to "have no other gods" (Exodus 20:3) before the Lord. On a spiritual level, Swedenborg says, *other gods* could be anything that we love or value above all else: money, power, reputation, or simply our own ego.

The golden calf, of course, angered God and Moses. Moses came down from the mountain and flung the tablets on the ground, breaking them. He begged God for forgiveness on behalf of the people, and God allowed him to return to Mount Sinai. Finally, after another forty days and nights on the mountain—the number forty, Swedenborg tells us, means a time of trial and testing—Moses comes back down with the stone tablets restored and his face shining.

An old cartoon shows two lawyers in front of an immense law library, with one saying to the other: "To think it all started with the Ten Commandments." In Swedenborg's theology, the commandments are that fundamental and that profound, speaking not just to the children of Israel but to all people, for all time. He writes: "In a brief encapsulation [the Ten Commandments] included all the elements of religion that provide for God's connection to us and our connection to God. Therefore the Ten Commandments were the holiest thing of all" (*True Christianity* §283).

The spiritual meaning of the Ten Commandments, as Swedenborg describes it, adds layers and layers to their application to life. The commandment against killing is not only about physical killing but about harming people in any way, with words as well as with weapons. The commandment against stealing applies not only to property but also to a person's good name.

If people choose to love and follow God by obeying his commandments, Swedenborg says, they are choosing to rise above a life focused on self and the world and to become spiritual. The final step on this journey comes in Joshua 1, when Joshua, the son of Moses, prepares the children of Israel to cross over the river Jordan to possess their promised land.

To understand the meaning of the river Jordan, we need to go back to Genesis 13, when Abram and his brother Lot had grown wealthy—and grown apart. There was so much strife between them, and they each had so many flocks and herds, that "the land could not sustain them" (6 [*Secrets of Heaven* §1567]). So they decided to separate. Abram chose to settle in the land of Canaan—the promised land for his descendants, the children of Israel. Lot chose to stay on the other side. The river became a dividing line, a real and symbolic boundary between them.

The conflict and separation of Abram and Lot depicts something that goes on inside each of us, Swedenborg says: the division between our external nature (all of our senses and the things of the world) and the internal, or spiritual, part of us (our soul).

The river Jordan, he says, represents a boundary between body and soul or between the inner, more spiritual parts of our mind and the outer part, which is more concerned with everyday life. Because of this, it is also symbolic that Jesus chose to be baptized in the

Jordan. Swedenborg explains that God wants to lead us through regeneration so that we can "cross the Jordan" into a higher, spiritual life.

The journey to become spiritual, he says, is what the forty years in the wilderness are all about. Through the trials and experiences of our life, we develop a spiritual conscience, with values we can rely on; or we turn away from the river's edge and stay in Egypt. It is our choice. But the more we choose to grow and develop spiritually, he says, the more we are enlightened and become like "the people who walked in darkness [and] have seen a great light" (Isaiah 9:2). Therefore crossing the Jordan and entering Canaan symbolizes turning our own hearts and minds toward God and away from the things of this world.

Swedenborg says that our journey begins like the children of Israel's—in the external, worldly land of Egypt as slaves to all that consumes us. The forty years of wandering through trials and temptations, led by God's pillars of cloud and fire, are how we get to the river Jordan and are able to cross into a spiritual land of milk and honey. The experiences of the children of Israel show how difficult the journey can be. That is especially true, Swedenborg tells us, if we are not connected to spiritual values and try to make our way with just the relatively dim light of this world. But however we journey, God is showing the way—if we are willing to see and be led.

This is a necessary journey for each of us, just as it was for the children of Israel, to grow into the kind of people God wants us to be. When we find a new direction, with the true north of a spiritual compass, that is when we are ready to cross the Jordan.

Just when the children of Israel are nearing the end of their journey, Moses says to them: "Remember the long way that the Lord your God has led you these forty years in the wilderness, in order to humble you, testing you to know what was in your heart, whether or not you would keep his commandments" (Deuteronomy 8:2). Only after Moses dies are they finally led across the Jordan by Joshua to the Promised Land.

One of the final exhortations from Moses to the children of Israel before Joshua delivered them to Canaan still speaks to us and our journey.

> Surely, this commandment that I am commanding you today is not too hard for you, nor is it too far away. It is not in heaven, that you should say, "Who will go up to heaven for us, and get it for us so that we may hear it and observe it?" Neither is it beyond the sea, that you should say, "Who will cross to the other side of the sea for us, and get it for us so that we may hear it and observe it?" No, the word is very near to you; it is in your mouth and in your heart for you to observe.
>
> See, I have set before you today life and prosperity, death and adversity. If you obey the commandments of the Lord your God that I am commanding you today, by loving the Lord your God, walking in his ways, and observing his commandments, decrees, and ordinances, then you shall live and become numerous, and the Lord your God will bless you in the land that you are entering to possess. . . . I call heaven and earth to witness against you today that I have set before you life and death, blessings and curses. Choose life. (Deuteronomy 30:11–16, 19)

That is what underlies everything in the Bible, from Genesis through Revelation: Love God. Love your neighbor. Choose life, but choose not just the life of this world. Choose spiritual life—the life of heaven, the Promised Land.

6

THE NEW TESTAMENT: A NEW VISION OF GOD

I look upon all four gospels as thoroughly genuine, for there is in them the reflection of a greatness which emanated from the person of Jesus.

— Johann Wolfgang von Goethe

The Bible in all my perplexities and distresses has never failed to give me light and strength.

— Gen. Robert E. Lee

The New Testament is the best book that ever was or ever will be known in the world.

— Charles Dickens

The journey continues with the New Testament. But here, the tone and manner of teaching are different, and our relationship with God is potentially different.

For many Christians, the New Testament is easier than the Old Testament; it is easier to read, easier to understand, and easier to accept.

Instead of an apparently angry and vengeful God, there is Jesus and a message of love.

Instead of complex family dynamics, there are simple parables.

Instead of relentless wars and violence, there is a kinder, gentler approach.

Instead of ruthless kings, there are humble disciples.

Instead of the great and distant dramas of the children of Israel, Saul and David, and Elijah and Elisha, Christians are invited to embrace the joy of the Christmas story, ponder the personal impact of the Crucifixion, and exult in the triumph and promise of Easter.

It is the same God in the Old and New Testaments. God does not change. So why does everything seem so different?

In the Old Testament, Swedenborg says, the understanding of God was obscured by the people's blindness and ignorance. They saw him as though "through a glass darkly," as a verse from Corinthians goes. God appeared to be angry because that is what the people of the time expected to see. And that is the way the Old Testament is written. But in the New Testament, Swedenborg writes, God appears in the human form of Jesus Christ so that he can be seen and his love felt. He is speaking to us directly.

In the Old Testament, so full of laws and rituals, God can seem distant. In the New Testament, we see a more personal and personable God—merciful, healing, and kind. We have seen that the Old Testament can be challenging because of the way God often is portrayed as a distant, angry father, striking down those who do not obey. In the New Testament, we get the much gentler and more approachable Son of God. The difference, according to Swedenborg, is in the way we see and understand him, not in God himself. It is the same God teaching in both the Old and New Testaments according to our levels of understanding. It is significant that in the New Testament, the title most often given to Jesus by his disciples and followers is *rabbi,* which means teacher. He came on earth to teach, and through the stories preserved in the Bible, he is teaching still.

If we understand the inner spiritual sense of both the Old and New Testaments, Swedenborg says, we can see and know God and feel a closer relationship with him. A mother may appear angry to a child who is scolded for running into the street or for hitting a younger sibling. The child is fearful and sees anger, but the mother is acting from love. She is protecting her child and nurturing good values. The child usually comes to see and appreciate this, if not at the time. Swedenborg likewise describes the people of the Old Testament as childlike. They feared God and expected to be punished or condemned when they went against his commands. They saw him as angry because that is what they expected—like the misbehaving child who sees a parent in that moment as angry and not loving.

Just as the child eventually grows and becomes more mature, Swedenborg says, when God came into the world to live among the people as Jesus Christ, they could see his true nature and begin to love him back. The disciples he chose were simple fishermen who were not corrupted with false beliefs. They were innocent followers, open to learning lessons from Jesus—their teacher—and helping to spread those lessons among the people.

Swedenborg says that the main theme of the New Testament is the same as it is in the Old but that it is cast in more loving and relevant terms. The spiritual meaning seems closer to the surface and to our lives, especially in stories and sayings that describe healing the sick and loving one's neighbor. The Old Testament may be compared to a geode, with its glittering core hidden inside a rough stone surface. The New Testament is more like a diamond; it already sparkles, but the more we hold it up to the light, the more radiance we see. The emphasis, Swedenborg explains, is consistent in both testaments: we have the freedom to accept God or reject him.

We begin our exploration of the inner meaning of the New Testament with an overview of the four Gospels. Swedenborg writes that the four Gospels, plus the book of Revelation, have an internal spiritual sense. The rest of the New Testament, he says, is also full of important teachings, but those other books are more literal in their meaning. After an overview of the Gospels, we consider one of the most popular and beloved accounts in the New Testament—the Sermon on the Mount—adding spiritual depth to its clear moral teachings. It illustrates how Jesus spoke at that time and still speaks to us today—through parables, which are simple but challenging stories that convey a spiritual principle. This is part of the overall biblical message about what God wants and expects from us, how he helps us form a relationship with him, and how we can follow him through our lives and into heaven.

The Four Gospels

One thing made quickly apparent in the New Testament is the shift of authority from intermediaries—Abraham, Moses, and the Patriarchs—to Jesus Christ himself as teacher, letting us know what he expects from us.

Gospel means good news. The books of Matthew, Mark, Luke, and John—the four Gospels—are attributed to evangelists of the same name who spread the good news about God coming down to earth. They were written between 60 and 90 AD because eyewitness accounts of the life of Jesus Christ were dying out and needed to be preserved. The written Gospels came about because in 70 AD the

Romans destroyed the Second Temple, a center of Jewish religious life in the city of Jerusalem. The Jews and newly forming Christians fled for their lives. This diaspora also marked the early stages of Christianity as an independent religion, as various groups began to establish churches across the Roman Empire.

Most editions of the Bible start with the Gospel of Matthew and then proceed to Mark, Luke, and John, although scholars generally agree that Mark actually was written first. Once all four were brought together and canonized at the beginning of the Catholic Church, Matthew was placed first because that particular Gospel emphasizes the primacy of Peter: "You are Peter, and on this rock I will build my church" (Matthew 16:18).

But the order of the Gospels, Swedenborg says, is not as important as what they say and how they say it. Each has a different and distinct viewpoint and approach. Matthew is literary and poetic. Mark can sound almost harsh by comparison; he is a straightforward biographer. Luke is thought to be an educated man who emphasized the proper portrayal of history. John, on the other hand, focuses on theology and philosophy.

Jesus primarily taught through parables and miracles. There are some thirty parables in Matthew, Mark, and Luke, but there are none in John, who talks instead about "signs." Matthew and Luke are the favorite Gospels of many Christians because they portray both the human and divine aspects of Jesus. John focuses only on the divine aspect. He is more doctrinal and less personal. Each Gospel has a distinct perspective on the life and work of Jesus. Each has its own richness. Swedenborg says we need all four to appreciate the intrinsic harmony within them.

MARK is the most realistic in his depiction of Jesus's life and actions. He is not warm and poetic, so people often don't relate to him as easily. He focuses on Jesus's miracles and his power rather than on the less dramatic parables. He stresses the humanity of Jesus—even Jesus's apparent anger, frustration, weariness, and hunger. Mark is all about faith and perseverance.

His Gospel opens not with the birth of Jesus and the Christmas story but with John the Baptist. Instead of angels and shepherds, we have "the voice of one crying out in the wilderness," preparing the way of the Lord and preaching "a baptism of repentance for the forgiveness of sins" (Mark 1:3, 4). By contrast, Matthew places the account of John the Baptist after the birth of Jesus; he has John the Baptist proclaiming that the kingdom of God is at hand and warning the Pharisees and Sadducees of the coming judgment (Matthew 3:2, 7–9). Swedenborg says this also illustrates how the Gospels complement each other.

MATTHEW expands on the framework of the life of Jesus laid out in Mark. The shift from Moses—as the intermediary who brought the original set of laws to the children of Israel—to the authority of Jesus Christ is established in the Sermon on the Mount (Matthew 5, 6, 7). Jesus speaks from his own authority, repeating with each instruction: "You have heard that it was said . . . but I say to you . . ." This, Swedenborg says, is when we begin to see and relate to the human qualities of Jesus as teacher. He was teaching his followers how to be disciples (students) and then to become apostles (teachers); and through their record of his words, he still is teaching us how to live our lives with higher spiritual values.

Matthew introduces us to Jesus's favorite teaching device with the parable of the sower (which is repeated in Mark and Luke). When the disciples ask why he speaks to these simple people in parables, he says, "To you it has been given to know the secrets of the kingdom of heaven, but to them it has not been given," and "seeing they do not perceive, and hearing they do not listen, nor do they understand" (Matthew 13:11, 13). Parables are like riddles, deliberately framed to make people think before they can understand.

Matthew describes Jesus giving his disciples the authority to "cure the sick, raise the dead, cleanse the lepers"—to give people the truth they hungered for, as Swedenborg puts it. But at the same time, Jesus also gently admonishes those disciples, saying, "You received without payment; give without payment" (Matthew 10:8).

Before describing the crucifixion of Jesus, Matthew gives the first foretelling of the Last Judgment and the Second Coming, which are more fully elaborated in the book of Revelation.

Matthew concludes with "the commissioning of the disciples," which can also be seen as a call to all the faithful to become disciples in his name. Such followers are asked to hear the echo of freely sharing with others what has been given to them: "Go therefore and make disciples of all nations, baptizing them in the name of the Father and of the Son and of the Holy Spirit, and teaching them to obey everything that I have commanded you." This Gospel ends with the enduring promise that the Bible contains for all believers: "And remember, I am with you always, to the end of the age" (Matthew 28:19–20).

LUKE writes like a historian, devoted to accuracy, and declares his purpose in his opening verses: "Since many have undertaken to set down an orderly account of the events that have been fulfilled among us . . . I too decided, after investigating everything carefully from the very first, to write an orderly account" (Luke 1:1, 3). He begins his account with Zacharias and Elizabeth, the conception of John the Baptist, and the angel appearing to Mary to tell her that "the Lord is with you" (Luke 1:28).

Luke is also thought to be the author of the book immediately following the Gospels, the Acts of the Apostles. Swedenborg suggests that it's good to read both together because they fulfill Luke's mission of spreading the teachings of Jesus and portray Jesus as the fulcrum of human history.

Historians focus on kings and rulers and their influence for good or evil in the world. Luke portrays Jesus as the greatest king—ruler of the kingdom of God—because of his divinity and his loving leadership of the people.

Women played a major role in the life of Jesus and the development of the early Christian church. This is seen most clearly in Luke, particularly in the roles of Elizabeth and Mary.

In the Easter story, Mark and Matthew both focus on the Crucifixion, but Luke focuses more on the empty tomb and the Resurrection.

He speaks to the ultimate promise of life after death and also to the promise that redemption and salvation are for all—not just for the favored few or the baptized but for everyone who looks to God and wants to be saved.

JOHN is unique among the Gospels. He concentrates not on history or biography but on theology, writing about the divinity of Christ. He surely was aware of the other Gospels, which all have similarities, but he did not seem to want to repeat them. His theme, purpose, and style are different. He had his own mission.

In his prologue, John focuses on God coming to earth as the Word. Jesus is portrayed as purely divine, coming not so much as a man but as the light of life: "In the beginning was the Word, and the Word was with God, and the Word was God" (John 1:1). What follows is John the Baptist testifying that Jesus is the Messiah; instead of describing the birth of Jesus and its impact on the people, John jumps straight to Jesus's ministry.

More than the other Gospels, John asks his readers to think spiritually. He does this partly by speaking of "signs"—such as purging the temple and delivering the woman accused of adultery—rather than focusing on miracles or parables. These signs, Swedenborg says, signify the divinity of Jesus.

John concludes the four Gospels with a hint of all that was left out in the life and teachings of Jesus Christ: "But there are also many other things that Jesus did; if every one of them were written down, I suppose that the world itself could not contain the books that would be written" (John 21:25).

So how and why did Matthew, Mark, Luke, and John decide what to include and what not to? Swedenborg's answer is that every word in the Gospels—as with everything else in the Bible—is there solely because it has spiritual meaning in addition to the literal sense.

We see this early in the Gospel of Matthew, with the first recorded example of Jesus as a teacher: the Sermon on the Mount. And within these beloved, simple words are spiritual lessons that still resonate in our lives today.

The Sermon on the Mount

For the first thirty years of his life on earth, Jesus lived quietly as a child and a carpenter's apprentice. We know almost nothing about his childhood, except that Luke says, "The child grew and became strong, filled with wisdom; and the favor of God was upon him" (Luke 2:40).

When he was twelve, Jesus went with his parents to Jerusalem for the feast of the Passover. As they returned home, they traveled for a day, "assuming that he was in the group of travelers," before realizing he was not with them. They hurried back to Jerusalem, no doubt sick with worry, and found him in the temple "sitting among the teachers, listening to them and asking them questions. And all who heard him were amazed at his understanding and his answers" (Luke 2:44, 46–47).

Luke depicts Jesus as preparing for the ministry and miracles that would fill the last three years of his brief life. In this account, Jesus was doing what he asks us to do—to elevate our nature by developing spiritually as well as mentally and physically. When kings assume leadership, they assert political and physical power. Through the three years of his ministry and leading the people, Swedenborg says, Jesus's power was spiritual and divine.

Everything Jesus did was about love and healing, both physically and spiritually. He was teaching then—and still is teaching today—to love, obey, and serve him by loving and serving our neighbor.

His public ministry, and his mission on earth, began with the Sermon on the Mount.

Even people who had been aware of Jesus as a special child must have been surprised to hear him suddenly teaching with such power, authority, and insight.

The sermon probably took Jesus about twenty minutes to deliver, just as long as it takes to read or hear it now, but its simple words have the power to transform lives. The power is in how people give the words meaning in their lives.

As Swedenborg puts it:

> [Union with the Lord] does not happen by simply knowing or by simply understanding or even by simply being wise; it happens by a life that is one with these states.... The more closely we are united to the Lord, the happier we become. (*Divine Providence* §§33, 37)

Jesus chose to begin the Sermon on the Mount with a litany of those who are blessed, today known as the Beatitudes. In the process, he made his listeners aware of the blessings in their lives—even if some of these blessings may not always feel as such:

> "Blessed are the poor in spirit, for theirs is the kingdom of heaven.
> Blessed are those who mourn, for they will be comforted.
> Blessed are the meek, for they will inherit the earth.
> Blessed are those who hunger and thirst for righteousness, for they will be filled.
> Blessed are the merciful, for they will receive mercy.
> Blessed are the pure in heart, for they will see God.
> Blessed are the peacemakers, for they will be called children of God.
> Blessed are those who are persecuted for righteousness' sake, for theirs is the kingdom of heaven.
> Blessed are you when people revile you and persecute you and utter all kinds of evil against you falsely on my account. Rejoice and be glad, for your reward is great in heaven, for in the same way they persecuted the prophets who were before you." (Matthew 5:3–12)

You may think, "Wait a minute. Is it really a blessing to be poor in spirit, to mourn, to be meek, to be persecuted? Doesn't our culture tell us, 'blessed are the powerful, the rich, and the beautiful'?" But as Jesus often did with his parables and teachings, he is challenging us to think more deeply.

When we experience grief or suffering, we may have a greater appreciation for happiness and may even be motivated to make changes in our lives that will make us happier. We don't feel blessed if we are hungry, but on a spiritual level, we are blessed when we hunger for truth. Swedenborg teaches that the more we come to realize that all blessings come from God, the more we approach him from humility and love; and the more we do what we can to help our neighbor, the more we will be peaceful and happy.

The fact that merciful peacemakers are blessed reinforces the concept that it is better to give than to receive. We may glimpse the illusion of happiness when we indulge our wants, but it doesn't last. We are more likely to feel happiness when we are doing things for others—for family, for friends, even for strangers.

There may be plenty of times in life when we proclaim, "Life isn't fair!" or we wonder, "Why does God let it happen?" A loved one may get cancer. People die in wars and accidents. Women and children are abused. Innocent people suffer. There's an old saying: "Life is a grindstone, and whether it grinds you down or polishes you up depends on what you're made of." Swedenborg tells us that if trust in God is what we're made of—trust that his providence is always leading toward good, no matter what the appearance—then we can stand up to anything.

Remember the story of Joseph in Genesis: As a young man he was sold into slavery by his brothers and was then thrown into prison in Egypt. Joseph was a good boy. He was the favorite of his father, and that created jealousy among his brothers. There was nothing fair in how he was treated.

Swedenborg explains that the story of Joseph is really about God and our relationship with him. If Joseph had not endured slavery and prison, he never would have risen to become an important advisor to the pharaoh in Egypt, where he was not only reconciled with his brothers but was able to save them and thousands more from starvation. His persecution became a blessing. It is the same with us. We may dwell on the past and feel victimized, Swedenborg says, but what feels like struggle and persecution may turn into a blessing, with God's providence and guidance.

The Beatitudes are followed with:

> "You are the salt of the earth; but if salt has lost its taste, how can its saltiness be restored? It is no longer good for anything, but is thrown out and trampled under foot.

"You are the light of the world. A city built on a hill cannot be hid. No one after lighting a lamp puts it under the bushel basket, but on the lampstand, and it gives light to all in the house. In the same way, let your light shine before others, so that they may see your good works and give glory to your Father in heaven." (Matthew 5:13–16)

Salt, Swedenborg says, corresponds to truth that "flavors" goodness. The idea is that we can't just have truth in our lives; it must be put to work to be meaningful. The combination of goodness and truth is what makes it possible for us to overcome temptation and be regenerated.

Swedenborg describes regeneration as a process in which our inner self is reborn. What helps us get to that point, he says, are our ideals, our vision of what it takes to become a better person. Light—whether a candle in the darkness, a beacon in a lighthouse, or a distant star—is a symbol of the ideals that inspire us and in turn can lift others.

The guide that is given for our lives and for regeneration is the Ten Commandments; and in the Sermon on the Mount, Jesus underscores their importance and elaborates on them:

"Do not think that I have come to abolish the law or the prophets; I have come not to abolish but to fulfill. . . . Whoever breaks one of the least of these commandments, and teaches others to do the same, will be called least in the kingdom of heaven; but whoever does them and teaches them will be called great in the kingdom of heaven." (Matthew 5:17, 19)

In the verses that come after, we see part of the biblical basis for Swedenborg's interpretation of the spiritual meaning within the Ten Commandments:

"You have heard that it was said to those of ancient times, 'You shall not murder'; and 'whoever murders shall be liable to judgment.' But I say to you that if you are angry with a brother or sister, you will be liable to judgment; and if you insult a brother or sister, you will be liable to the council; and if you say, 'You fool,' you will be liable to the hell of fire." (Matthew 5:21–22)

To be angry with someone, to talk behind a person's back, to spread malicious gossip, to be overly critical—all of these actions can effectively kill a relationship. You may know what that feels like, whether you've been at the receiving end or the giving end. This is not what God wants, Swedenborg tells us; he wants us to love him and our neighbor, which is why he commands us to be kind and loving in our relationships.

Jesus also teaches that committing adultery can include an action as simple as looking at a woman with lust in one's heart. And he adds, "If your right eye causes you to sin, tear it out and throw it away; it is better for you to lose one of your members than for your whole body to be thrown into hell" (Matthew 5:29). This is a warning, Swedenborg says, that we are responsible—and judged—not just for what we do but also for our intentions. Would we sin if we knew we could get away with it? We need to be aware of our intentions, he warns, because they reveal what we love and who we really are.

There is a change from the harsh laws of the Old Testament, however, when Jesus says, "You have heard that it was said, 'An eye for an eye and a tooth for a tooth.' But I say to you, Do not resist an evildoer. But if anyone strikes you on the right cheek, turn the other also" (Matthew 5:38–39).

Beginning when we are children, we are consumed with fairness, especially as to how we are treated. Fairness is important. But the emphasis here is on goodness, not fairness; it's about treating others with kindness and compassion. Jesus is asking us not to give in to our instincts for retaliation and to spread our pain to others but instead to be positive and healing. No matter how justified we may feel in lashing out, that type of action will not help a relationship. With a kind and loving approach and open communication, we can move forward instead of backward.

Jesus goes so far as to tell us, "Love your enemies and pray for those who persecute you" (Matthew 5:44). Swedenborg reflects this when he writes, "Jehovah God—the Lord—never curses anyone, is never angry at anyone, never leads anyone into crisis. . . . Nothing of the sort could ever come from the fountain of mercy, peace, and goodness" (*Secrets of Heaven* §245).

The Sermon on the Mount contains another pivotal lesson in the form of the Lord's Prayer:

> "Our Father in heaven,
> hallowed be your name.
> Your kingdom come.
> Your will be done,
> on earth as it is in heaven.
> Give us this day our daily bread.
> And forgive us our debts,
> as we also have forgiven our debtors.
> And do not bring us to the time of trial,
> but rescue us from the evil one." (Matthew 6:9–13)

Swedenborg says that whenever he recited the Lord's Prayer,

> I have had a clear sensation of being raised up toward the Lord by a sort of magnetism. . . . I was aware of the Lord's inflow into every word of the prayer and therefore into every single thought sparked in my mind by the prayer's message.
>
> This inflow did not occur the same way one time as another but in indescribably varied ways, which showed how infinitely much each detail of the prayer held within it. It also showed that the Lord was present in all the details. (*Secrets of Heaven* §6476)

People who pray regularly may do so first as an expression of hope and ultimately as an expression of trust. When they say with conviction, "Your will be done," they are trusting God with their lives and salvation. They generally feel spiritually mature and at peace.

A much-loved prayer from the Old Testament echoes the teachings from the Sermon on the Mount: "He has told you, O mortal, what is good; and what does the Lord require of you but to do justice, and to love kindness, and to walk humbly with your God?" (Micah 6:8).

One of the most familiar and cherished prayers about personal change is attributed to the thirteenth-century friar St. Francis of Assisi, and it was first published in France in 1912:

Lord, make me an instrument of thy peace.
Where there is hatred, let me sow love;
Where there is injury, pardon;
Where there is doubt, faith;
Where there is despair, hope;
Where there is darkness, light;
Where there is sadness, joy.
O divine Master,
Grant that I may not so much seek to be consoled
As to console,
To be understood as to understand,
To be loved as to love;
For it is in giving that we receive;
It is in pardoning that we are pardoned;
It is in dying to self that we are born to eternal life.

Swedenborg teaches that prayer is not just something we do in quiet moments of reflection; it enters into every facet of our life and affects our connection with God:

Worship does not consist in prayers and in external devotion, but in a life of charity. . . . Spiritual affection is what is called charity towards the neighbor; to be in that affection is true worship; praying is what proceeds. (*Apocalypse Explained* §325:3)

The admonition that follows the Lord's Prayer to "forgive others their trespasses [as] your heavenly Father will also forgive you" (Matthew 6:14) calls on us to make choices from a higher, spiritual plane. It means choosing what turns us toward God—love, compassion, kindness—and not the things that turn us away, such as anger, lust, hatred, contempt, cruelty, and revenge. It means living fully in the moment, but always with an awareness that we live for eternity. It's said that "you can't take it with you." If we understand "it" in that expression to be our possessions, then that's true. But we can and do take whatever belongs to our character: the things that we love, value, and believe. What really matters is that our choices are based on what we value most.

We may long for the peace of heaven in our life and in the world. We won't find it in money and things, though. It comes as we let trust infuse our lives. "Peace holds within itself trust in the Lord, the trust that he governs all things and provides all things, and that he leads toward an end that is good" (*Secrets of Heaven* §8455).

With a spiritual focus and trust in God we need not worry about what happens during our life on earth, but should be content, like the lilies of the field. "Indeed your heavenly Father knows that you need all these things. But strive first for the kingdom of God and his righteousness, and all these things will be given to you as well" (Matthew 6:32–33).

Jesus offers hope that it is not so hard as we might think to live the life that leads to heaven. It's a matter of choosing what we know to be good and rejecting what may seem enticing but is in fact contrary to the commandments. Once we get used to thinking this way, Jesus assures us, "My yoke is easy, and my burden is light" (Matthew 11:30).

Taking on that yoke depends on the choices we make. We may find it easy, for instance, to judge others—to find fault and feel superior. But we are counseled: "Do not judge, so that you may not be judged. For with the judgment you make you will be judged, and the measure you give will be the measure you get" (Matthew 7:1–2).

This teaching arises again a few verses later in the profound simplicity of the Golden Rule: "In everything do to others as you would have them do to you; for this is the law and the prophets" (Matthew 7:12). We all want to be treated with kindness and respect, but may not always remember to treat others that way in moments of anger or wanting our own way.

Swedenborg says it comes down to who you love more, yourself or your neighbor. He offers a description—which can be either inspiring or chilling—of how this is manifested when people die and awaken in the spiritual world:

Those who lack all kindness radiate hatred from every pore. They want to examine and in fact judge everyone and crave nothing more than to find evil, constantly bent as they are on condemning, punishing, and torturing others.

Those who are guided by kindness, on the other hand, hardly even notice evil in another but pay attention instead to everything good and true in the person. When they do find anything bad or false, they put a good interpretation on it. This is a characteristic of all angels—one they acquire from the Lord, who bends everything bad toward good. (*Secrets of Heaven* §1079:2)

The way to become an angel in heaven, he adds, is simply to begin living as an angel in this world, with an attitude of kindness and charity. Living with judgment, anger, and a lack of kindness toward others is not choosing to be an angel. "No one can become an angel or get to heaven unless he or she arrives bringing along some angelic quality from the world" (*Divine Providence* §60).

The Sermon on the Mount ends with a story that ties all of these lessons together: the foolish man who builds his house on the sand and the wise man who builds his house on a rock. Part of the message, Swedenborg teaches, is that each of us is building a spiritual house in our own mind through the choices we make in this life, and that house will become our home once our soul passes to heaven or hell. The house built on a rock withstands the storms and does not fall because it rests on the foundation of God's truth. The house of the foolish man, built on the sand—with nothing of truth to anchor it—could not stand, "and great was its fall" (Matthew 7:27). Building our house on a rock does not make us immune to the storms of life, however. The rains, floods, and winds beat upon both houses, just as we all experience challenges throughout the course of our life.

When Jesus completed his Sermon on the Mount, "the crowds were astounded at his teaching, for he taught them as one having authority, and not as their scribes" (Matthew 7:28–29). They were amazed at the power of his simple, profound words: Live with love and kindness and integrity. Live with a sense of the eternal within our natural lives, of a spiritual depth within the literal words of sacred scripture. There will always be rain and floods and winds in life, but building our house on a rock is what makes the yoke easy and the burden light.

Teaching through Parables

The Sermon on the Mount is the best known and most prolonged example of Jesus speaking to us in a way that is different from that of the prophets of the Old Testament. He continues to do this throughout the New Testament, particularly through parables.

Parables are like Aesop's fables. They are simple stories, sometimes clearly understood, sometimes baffling, but always with a lesson. God is not just giving us neat answers that require no work on our own. He wants us to think and reflect, because that is how what we learn becomes a part of our lives.

There are a lot of good, commonsense applications for biblical parables, but Swedenborg adds a spiritual dimension to give us a new way of understanding these stories.

Matthew records a series of parables in chapter 13 of his gospel: the sower scattering seeds in stony ground, among thorns, and in good soil; tares planted among wheat; a tiny mustard seed growing into a tree; the leaven used in making bread; a treasure hidden in a field; the pearl of great price; and a net cast into the sea.

All of the parables, Swedenborg says, build on our relationship with God by illustrating situations that are like the kingdom of heaven. For instance, like the sower in the parable, God plants seeds of truth. What happens with those seeds depends on how we nurture that truth; it depends on whether we have "good ground" in our minds and are willing to hear the truth, accept it, and make it a part of our lives. Swedenborg says that even the smallest truth—like the tiny mustard seed—can grow God's kingdom within us.

In Luke we find the parable of the prodigal son, a classic lesson about fairness and goodness that takes on even richer meaning when Swedenborg interprets its spiritual sense. This is the story of a son who leaves home for a far country and "squandered his property in dissolute living" (Luke 15:13). His responsible brother stays home and works hard.

When the prodigal son has spent all that he has and faces famine, he slinks home, chastened for sinning against both his father and heaven and ready to live as just a hired servant. But his father celebrates his return, killing the fatted calf for a feast. The faithful son, who has served his father all these years, is angry that his irresponsible brother is feted while he never got any appreciation for his service.

His father says to him, "Son, you are always with me, and all that is mine is yours. But we had to celebrate and rejoice, because this brother of yours was dead and has come to life; he was lost and has been found" (Luke 15:31–32).

It makes sense that the father is happy to welcome home his "lost" son, but still it doesn't seem fair to the brother who has been responsible yet taken for granted. Swedenborg elaborates on the internal meaning of the story: The prodigal son represents everyone who has been given spiritual riches in the form of a knowledge of goodness and truth. His return to his father represents the realization by faithful people that they need their own father—God—in order to live spiritually. When he comes home, the gifts he receives represent the beginning of a deeper spiritual life, the process of inner rebirth that Swedenborg calls regeneration (*Apocalypse Explained* §279:6, *Secrets of Heaven* §9391:6).

A different parable concerning a rich man also challenges our perceptions. When the rich man asks Jesus what he should do to inherit eternal life, he is feeling good about himself, proclaiming that he has been keeping the commandments. But he is dismayed when Jesus says he still lacks one thing: "Go, sell what you own, and give the money to the poor, and you will have treasure in heaven; then come, follow me" (Mark 10:21). And Jesus reinforces this message by telling his disciples, "It is easier for a camel to go through the eye of a needle than for someone who is rich to enter the kingdom of God" (Mark 10:25).

This has troubled many good and wealthy people, but again, Swedenborg's interpretation of the internal sense sheds new light on this story:

> "The rich person" here means the rich in both senses, natural and spiritual. Rich people in the natural sense are people who have abundant wealth and set their hearts on it, while in a spiritual sense they are people who are amply supplied with insights and knowledge (for these are spiritual wealth) and who want to use them to get themselves into heavenly and ecclesiastical circles by their own intellect. Since this is contrary to the divine design, it says that it is easier for a camel to get through the eye of a needle. On this level of meaning, a camel means our cognitive and informational level in general, and the eye of a needle means spiritual truth. (*Heaven and Hell* §365:3)

Again, we see that the parable is not literally about rich people but is about people who rely on the wealth of knowledge they have accumulated throughout their lives. In order to become spiritual people, they must let go of what they think they know and seek a higher authority:

> "To sell all that he had" signifies that he should relinquish the things . . . that were his own *(proprium)*, which were loving self and the world more than God . . . and "to follow the Lord" signifies to acknowledge him only and to be led by him. (*Apocalypse Explained* §934:2)

One of the best-known parables in the New Testament is the story of the good Samaritan. As the story goes, a lawyer also asked what he should do to inherit eternal life. When Jesus asked him what was written in the law, he correctly answered, "You shall love the Lord your God with all your heart, and with all your soul, and with all your strength, and with all your mind; and your neighbor as yourself" (Luke 10:27).

Then the lawyer pressed on and asked, "Who is my neighbor?"

This is when Jesus told the parable of the good Samaritan. There was a man who was attacked by thieves, beaten, and left for dead. A priest passed by on the other side of the road. A Levite stopped to look, but he also passed by. But the Samaritan took compassion on the man, bandaged his wounds, put him on his own animal, and took him to an inn, where he paid the innkeeper to take care of him. When Jesus asked which of these three was neighbor to this needy man, the rich man said, "The one who showed him mercy." Then Jesus said to him, "Go and do likewise" (Luke 10:37).

Just like the rich man, we get the meaning. But Swedenborg enlarges on it:

> The Lord's parable about the Samaritan shows that there are degrees of love for our neighbor. The Samaritan had mercy on the person who had been wounded by robbers—a person whom both the priest and the Levite had seen and yet passed by. When the Lord asked which of the three seemed to have been a neighbor, the reply was "the one who had mercy" (Luke 10:30–37).
>
> We read that we are to love the Lord God above all things, and our neighbor as ourselves (Luke 10:27). To love our neighbor as ourselves means not despising our neighbors in comparison with ourselves. It means treating them justly and not judging them wrongfully. . . . This is how people who love heaven love their neighbor. People who love the world, however, love their neighbor on a worldly basis for a worldly benefit. People who love themselves love their neighbor in a selfish way for a selfish benefit. (*True Christianity* §§410:3–411)

One last story with clear enough meaning in the literal words but even fuller meaning in the spiritual sense is the parable of the talents. In this story in Matthew, a man traveling to a far country called his servants together. To one, he gave five talents (a sum of money); to another, two; and to a third, just one talent. The master wanted to see what his servants had done with their talents by the time he returned.

The one given five talents had traded with them and earned five more. The man given two also had doubled them. But the servant given just one talent was afraid of losing it and buried it in the ground so that he could be sure to return it.

When the master returned, he was pleased with the first two servants and said to each of them: "Well done, good and trustworthy [servant]; you have been trustworthy in a few things, I will put you in charge of many things; enter into the joy of your master" (Matthew 25:21 and 23). These words often are repeated in eulogies to honor those who have led good and productive lives with the "talents" God gave them.

But the master chastised as a "wicked and lazy [servant]" (Matthew 25:26) the one who hid his talent and returned it unused, and he ordered that his talent be given to the other who had ten. "For to all those who have, more will be given, and they will have an abundance; but from those who have nothing, even what they have will be taken away" (Matthew 25:29).

This may seem harsh, even cruel. The man with the one talent was afraid to risk losing everything. He made sure he would give back what he had been given, even if it was unused. But looking beyond the literal meaning of the story, Swedenborg tells us that the talents represent goodness within us. People who work hard to increase their own goodness on behalf of the Lord—so they can help to bring his love into the world—and not for their own sake will be abundantly rewarded. On the other hand, people who hide their goodness away and make no effort to put it into action, let alone encourage it to grow, will ultimately lose it all.

> Whatever we have acquired in this world stays with us. We take it with us after death, where it is increased and filled out, all within the level of our own affection and desire for what is true and good, and not beyond that level. People who have had little affection and desire accept little, but still as much as they can accept on their own level. People who have had great affection

and desire accept much. The actual level of affection and desire is like a measure that is filled to the brim. This means more for people whose measure is great and less for people whose measure is small. This is because the love to which affection and desire belong accepts everything that suits it, so the amount of love determines the amount of receptivity. This is the meaning of the Lord's words, "To all who have, it will be given, and they will have more abundantly" (Matthew 13:12; 25:29). (*Heaven and Hell* §349)

The message of many of the parables, and indeed the Bible itself, can be encapsulated in this observation from Swedenborg:

The Lord did not create the universe for his own sake but for the sake of people he would be with in heaven. By its very nature, spiritual love wants to share what it has with others, and to the extent that it can do so, it is totally present, experiencing its peace and bliss. (*Divine Providence* §27:2)

It is all about God's love, his constant effort to raise us up to be conjoined with him in heaven, and the call for us to repent and follow him—but always being left in freedom to choose.

Swedenborg explains that the New Testament indeed gives us a new vision of God. He is no longer the distant, sometimes angry God of the Old Testament but a visible God—one who has come down to earth so that people might know him and see him in a new way. He wants us to love and understand him and to feel his presence in our lives. Building a personal relationship with him, Swedenborg says, is the continuing blessing within our spiritual journey.

We see this all the more clearly in the special accounts of Jesus's birth, death, and resurrection, which are generally well known but offer so much more on the spiritual level.

7

CHRISTMAS AND EASTER: A NEW UNDERSTANDING

The only blind person at Christmastime is he who has not Christmas in his heart.

— Helen Keller

Then the Grinch thought of something he hadn't before. What if Christmas, he thought, doesn't come from a store? What if Christmas, perhaps, means a little bit more?

— Dr. Seuss

The resurrection gives my life meaning and direction and the opportunity to start over no matter what my circumstances.

— Robert Flatt

Easter says you can put truth in the grave, but it won't stay there.

— Clarence W. Hall

Christmas and Easter are the holidays that celebrate Jesus's birth and his death and resurrection, and these are probably the best-known and most-loved stories in the Bible. They are the two most holy and treasured holidays for Christians. Every year, they speak to the lives of people who hold them sacred.

In modern times, those celebrations have been confounded by Santa Claus and the Grinch, the Easter Bunny and egg hunts, and a grotesque commercialism overlaying it all. The core messages, however, remain strong.

The story of Jesus's birth appears in Matthew (1:18–2:23) and Luke (1:26–38; 2:1–20). It begins with an angel appearing to Mary, telling her that "the Lord is with you" (Luke 1:28) and that she will give birth to the Son of God. The Christ child is born in a simple stable, adored by shepherds, worshipped by wise men, feared by Herod.

Christians believe that Jesus Christ came into the world to save all people—Christian and non-Christian alike—and to lead us to peace and heaven. They celebrate Christmas with lights and gifts because they see God coming as "a new light" into the world with the gift of hope.

Easter can be both troubling and triumphant. Some Christians still cringe when they hear the story of how Jesus Christ, the Son of God who preached and practiced love to all, was betrayed and crucified. But the story also says that three days later, on Easter morning, he rose from the dead as he had promised and gave to us all the gift of everlasting life. His triumph can be seen as our triumph: a victory over hell—or "hells," as Swedenborg would say—that makes heaven possible for all who choose it.

The celebrations of Christmas and Easter are connected by themes of life and death, but they are separated by months and seasons. This is appropriate, because there is so much that happens in between—in the thirty-three years of Jesus's life and in the course of our own lives. But, Swedenborg says, these holy days should not be separated emotionally, because each is implicit in the other. Christmas is about why God came down to earth; Easter is the fulfillment of his purpose. Both speak to our own journey.

Christmas

Christmas may be the one time in the year that some people go to church—perhaps Easter and Thanksgiving, too. With all the insistent patterns of daily life and the distractions of the world around us, it is easy to miss the great mystery of Christmas. Peace often proves elusive amid the hubbub of the season, which is probably one reason why so many people seek comfort in the reverent atmosphere and joyous carols of a Christmas Eve service. For the faithful, this is when the enduring lessons that God is trying to teach can begin to come into focus.

If we read the Bible literally, the Christmas story appears in the Gospels of Matthew and Luke. However, Swedenborg writes that the whole of the Old Testament is a precursor to the Christmas story, that it is filled with prophecies and stories that herald God's coming on earth, even though those stories may seem to have nothing to do with it. Recall from chapter 3, for example, that Swedenborg interprets the first prophecy in the Bible as a reference to the coming of Jesus: "And I will put hostility between you and the woman and between your seed and her seed. He will trample you on the head and you will wound him on the heel" (Genesis 3:15 [*Secrets of Heaven* §250]).

Every story in the Old Testament, according to Swedenborg, is preparing—directly and indirectly—for God's birth on earth. Chief among these is the fall of civilization in the story of Noah and the Flood. That familiar tale is all about darkness and evil overwhelming what is good, which makes it necessary for God to wash away the evil and clear the way for a renewed spiritual understanding.

The theme of darkness also appears in the biblical tale of Jesus's birth. It is no accident that Jesus was born at night. The world had once again turned to spiritual darkness, full of ignorance, false beliefs, and evil. That is why Isaiah prophesied: "The people who walked in darkness have seen a great light; those who lived in a land of deep darkness—on them light has shined" (Isaiah 9:2). Darkness represents the false beliefs that had overcome the world. But as dark as that world was more than two thousand years ago, there were many good people ready to worship and to listen: Mary and Joseph, the shepherds and the wise men, the disciples who followed Jesus, and all the people moved by his teaching and example.

Swedenborg offers new insight that makes every detail of the Christmas story all the more beautiful, meaningful, and relevant to our lives. It begins with a question: why did the Son of God need to be born on earth? Among the various Christian denominations, the most common answer is, "To save the human race." Swedenborg's answer is similar on the surface, but he also describes a much more complex spiritual dynamic:

> The Lord came into the world for two main reasons: to move hell away from both angels and people; and to glorify his own human nature. Before the Lord's Coming, hell had grown so much that it was assaulting the angels of heaven. By placing itself between heaven and the world, hell had also become able to intercept the communication between the Lord and human beings on earth; as a result, no divine truth or goodness from the Lord was able to get through to human beings. A total damnation threatened the entire human race, and the angels of heaven would not have been able to maintain their integrity for long either.
>
> In order to move hell out of the way and to remove the impending threat of total damnation, the Lord came into the world, relocated hell, brought it under control, and made heaven accessible again, so that he would be able to be present among

people on earth and regenerate and save those who were living according to his commandments. (*True Christianity* §579:1–2)

Because of the corruption of the human race, Swedenborg explains, hell had become so strong that it upset the balance between itself and heaven. This meant that people were becoming less and less free to make their own choices. And this, he says, is what God coming on earth restored to us: our spiritual freedom to choose God and heaven.

Swedenborg says that too many people had forgotten God because they did not know him, so he came into the world to be seen and known as a human being and understood as a human God: "If you know me, you will know my Father also. From now on you do know him and have seen him" (John 14:7).

Jesus was born in a stable at night, among doubting and fearful people. He could have chosen to be born in a palace, immediately acclaimed as a king. Instead, as the familiar story goes, Mary and Joseph found no room in the inn and had to settle for a humble stable. The shepherds who were out tending their flocks, King Herod, and "all Jerusalem" were troubled by the signs and proclamations of the angels. To be viewed both as human and as God, Jesus needed to be seen not as a powerful king separate from the people but as an innocent, vulnerable baby—someone just like them. And as with us, it was necessary for him to be attacked and tempted by hell throughout his human life in order to triumph over it. In his triumph, he restored the balance between heaven and hell that is essential to our spiritual freedom.

As we have seen throughout the Old and New Testaments, there is spiritual meaning within every word of scripture, and this is also true of the biblical story of Jesus's birth.

That meaning, Swedenborg says, begins with John the Baptist. His birth to the elderly Elizabeth and Zacharias was just as much a miracle as was the birth of Jesus. The reason why John needed to come first is because his mission was baptism and repentance. John baptized people in the Jordan River, which is significant, as we saw in chapter 5, because the Jordan is the boundary that leads to the promised land of Canaan. By baptizing people in the Jordan, John was preparing the way for a new church—a new spiritual age.

The washing ritual of baptism also represents repentance or a cleansing of the spirit, with a promise to live by God's commandments. We all have to repent—to actively reject and avoid committing the sins outlined in those commandments—in order to enter heaven. When we reach this point in our lives, Swedenborg says, we are on the pathway to heaven, because we begin to become spiritual "and to be born anew with the help of the Lord" (*True Christianity* §530:3). That is why Jesus said to Nicodemus that "no one can see the kingdom of God without being born from above." And when Nicodemus asked how a man could be born when he is old, or enter a second time into his mother's womb, Jesus answered: "No one can enter the kingdom of God without being born of water and Spirit" (John 3:3, 5).

Talk of repentance and shunning evil may seem counter to the Christmas message of peace and happiness, but you can think of it as a process that makes peace and happiness possible. Swedenborg teaches that we should regularly and honestly examine ourselves, recognize and admit our failings, pray to God for help, and begin a new life. It is telling that our new year's resolutions to live better lives follow right after Christmas.

Jesus's birth was heralded by an angel who appeared as a bright star in the dark sky, so out of the ordinary that it frightened the shepherds to whom he announced the coming of the Messiah. Here again, we see imagery from the Old Testament. The earliest prophecies of God coming on earth pictured him as a star: "I see him, but not now; I behold him, but not near—a star shall come out of Jacob" (Numbers 24:17). Swedenborg explains that a star represents knowledge from heaven, especially knowledge about God. So there is a special meaning in having a star announce the birth of God.

Stars and light are recurring images in Old Testament prophecies and in the Christmas story. Swedenborg says that God is seen in heaven as the light of the sun, the source of everything good and true, and he adds,

> Because this light was no longer able to affect the human race, which had moved so far away from goodness and truth and therefore from the light, and had thrown itself into the dark, the Lord wished to clothe himself in true humanity by being born. In this way, he could shed light not only on our rational dimension but also on our earthly dimension. (*Secrets of Heaven* §3195:3)

One of the most popular people in the Christmas story, after Jesus himself, is Mary—not only because she was his mother but also because of her character and what she represents. When the angel came to tell her that "the Lord is with you" (Luke 1:28) and that she would bear the Son of God, she did not say, "Why me? I'm not even married. Can't you find someone else?" Instead, she said, "Here am I, the servant of the Lord; let it be with me according to your word" (Luke 1:38).

Linguists trace Mary's name to a root that means beloved, as in beloved of God. For modern seekers, she can represent anyone on a journey with God who longs to be guided by spiritual truth. All such people are like Mary—willingly accepting God's teachings and taking them into their lives.

Mary and Joseph can be seen as models for how we should respond to God's asking to be born in us. They both willingly took on their roles—she as a virgin mother and he as a man accepting rather than rejecting of her in her condition—because they had absolute trust in God. They were humble, innocent, and willing to be led by God rather than by their own will. They are enduring models for all who walk a God-centered spiritual path because only the innocent—those who follow God—can enter heaven.

That Jesus was born in a stable because, as the biblical account tells us, "there was no place for them in the inn" (Luke 2:7) is fraught with meaning. An inn, Swedenborg explains, represents a place to go for instruction, so *no place in the inn* means a state of affairs where the people in charge of instruction were not willing to receive divine truth.

The shepherds were told that they would find the babe wrapped in swaddling clothes and lying in a manger. Swaddling clothes, we are told, represent the truths that come when we experience divine love. The baby Jesus wrapped in swaddling clothes is a picture of the innocence people need to feel in approaching him. The shepherds had that innocence, and so they quickly overcame their fears and rushed to worship him.

The "good news of great joy" (Luke 2:10), which was the announcement of his birth, came first to simple shepherds "keeping watch over their flock by night" (Luke 2:8). That, Swedenborg says, is because shepherds are like spiritual guides—they lead us to what is good and true. It was the innocent who were able to truly receive and understand divine love and who would bring it to the people.

With humble hearts, the shepherds went up to Bethlehem to "see this thing that has taken place, which the Lord has made known to us." They went willingly, because faith and free will cannot be compelled. They "made known what had been told them" (Luke 2:15, 17).

The wise men of the Christmas story represent something different from what the shepherds represent. Since they were searching for the baby Jesus, they had a real sense of purpose in their journey. Swedenborg tells us that the wise men represent the knowledge of ancient people—the ones who understood correspondences—and therefore were able to read the signs around them and understand that God had come to earth.

Their gifts—gold, frankincense, and myrrh—are known to everyone who loves the Christmas story, but Swedenborg offers a new way to look at them. He says that these three things taken together represent all the different types of goodness that can come from loving others and having faith. These are the gifts that we should always offer to God from our own hearts.

Along with the wise men comes the dark side of the Christmas story—Herod. He is often pushed aside among all the happy, joyful aspects of the season, but he is essential to the story. Because of the prophecies about the coming of the Messiah—understood at that time to mean someone who would become king of the Jewish people—Herod feels his power threatened by this baby, and he orders the murder of every male child under the age of two, a horror beyond imagination. Having been warned in separate dreams, Joseph flees to Egypt with Mary and Jesus; and the wise men avoid Herod and Jerusalem, returning to their home by another way.

We could think of Herod as the evil that can come into our own minds. He is a reminder that even the joy and promise of Christmas come with an enduring challenge to stand up against the evil in the world—and in our lives. Herod was a roadblock in the wise men's journey, as he can be for ours. He was a threat to Jesus's mission, a mission that he had to confront throughout Jesus's life on earth.

God came into a world in chaos, Swedenborg teaches, to establish his presence with us. He was worshipped and loved even before he came into the world, but that worship happened amid a lot of doubt and blind faith—people going through the motions of worship without a real understanding of the Divine. Once God came to earth, he was real and became known. People were still free to reject him, as we are today, but they felt his presence in a different way.

There is a third version of the Christmas story, although it is not generally recognized as such because it never mentions Mary and the birth of Jesus; the angels; the shepherds; or the wise men. It is found in the Gospel of John, which begins:

> In the beginning was the Word, and the Word was with God,
> and the Word was God. . . . What has come into being in him
> was life, and the life was the light of all people. The light shines in
> the darkness, and the darkness did not overcome it. (1:1, 3–5)

God, who came to earth as the baby Jesus, still wants to be "born" with us. And that happens, Swedenborg says, whenever we read the Bible and turn to him with the innocence of the shepherds. Swedenborg explains that God's unconditional loving presence was not just something that visited the world two thousand years ago, but it is with us constantly. It heals and renews. He says that this is God's Christmas present to us—every day.

By coming to earth, God reopened the pathway to salvation and heaven. John the Baptist came to teach that first we must shun sin so that we can fully love God. Jesus teaches us then to love God and our neighbors, not ourselves. And so the loving gifts we give to others circle back as gifts to him. This is the true meaning of Christmas.

Easter

For people who live in the temperate climates with four distinct seasons, springtime is the metaphor for Easter: promise and denial. There is a constant push and pull between the lingering chill of winter and the warming sun that heralds the coming summer. Out of that struggle comes the triumph of nature—and a rebirth of the spirit.

We welcome the daffodils that light our landscapes and our hearts. We long for deliverance from the plagues of the world.

Like Christmas, Easter offers hope—for each of us and for the world. In roiling debates over morality and faith, we are challenged to elevate our minds. Easter offers perspective. It calls on people to reflect on its meaning and make it relevant to their lives by applying its spiritual message to the challenges we face.

The eternal message of Easter is found at the end of the Bible: "See, I am making all things new" (Revelation 21:5). Springtime is its theater. The soul is its mirror. A new spirit and a brighter future are its promise.

The drama begins with Jesus riding triumphantly into Jerusalem, hailed as a king. After all of the miracles he performed in his young life, all the suffering people he healed, all the wisdom he taught, and all the love he had shown, the wonder is why this heady celebration could within just a week collapse into betrayal, hatred, and crucifixion. And as with the story of Jesus's birth and everything else in the Bible, Swedenborg teaches, every aspect of the Easter story has meaning for our lives.

Jesus's triumphal entry into Jerusalem is recorded in all four Gospels: riding on a donkey before a "very large crowd" of people spreading their clothing and palm branches in his way and exclaiming, "Hosanna to the Son of David! Blessed is the one who comes in the name of the Lord" (Matthew 21:8, 9).

Swedenborg explains that the garments and the branches symbolize the way that spiritual truth is the foundation for God as a king in our lives. Knowing truth is one thing; acknowledging the divinity in it is another. Having faith in that truth—and living it—is most important of all. This, he says, is what regeneration is all about: learning truth, rejecting whatever is false, and living the life of heaven.

The people welcomed Jesus as a king, but they wanted him to be a king in the political sense, supplanting the despised Herod and the government of Rome. What they did not understand was that he came as the king of heaven, not as a worldly king.

Earlier, he had told the Pharisees, when they demanded to know when the kingdom of God would come, that "the kingdom of God is not coming with things that can be observed; nor will they say, 'Look, here it is!' or 'There it is!' For, in fact, the kingdom of God is among you" (Luke 17:20–21). They did not understand that heaven is a kingdom of God's love and that he wants his love to "rule" within us in the way we live our lives.

We are told that "as [Jesus] came near and saw the city, he wept over it" (Luke 19:41). This seems the opposite of what we would expect from someone who is being greeted as a king. Swedenborg says that Jesus's weeping was an act of love and grief, because Jerusalem represented not only a city but a state of mind—a state of mind where people's hearts were hardened and they weren't able to experience divine love or understand divine truth. Jesus understood that people wanted a social change, but the people did not understand that what was needed was a change in their hearts and minds. He wept because they were blinded by their own worldly lives and had no idea of his real purpose in coming down among them.

Listen to the pain in what he said next: "If you, even you, had only recognized on this day the things that make for peace! But now they are hidden from your eyes" (Luke 19:42). He knew what was still to come and wept, not for himself, but because the people still did not accept or believe what he taught.

Just five days after his triumphal entry, when he is about to be crucified and the women who love him are crying, he says to them: "Daughters of Jerusalem, do not weep for me, but weep for yourselves and for your children" (Luke 23:28). And as he was being crucified, he prayed with undying love, "Father, forgive them; for they do not know what they are doing" (Luke 23:34).

But between the welcoming of their "king" and the mocking crucifixion of the "King of the Jews" (Luke 23:37–38) came the confrontation that made his death inevitable.

In Matthew and Luke, the first thing Jesus did after entering Jerusalem was to purge the temple to drive out the money-changers for turning his "house of prayer" into a "den of robbers" (Luke 19:46). After purging the temple, the next thing he did seems curious. At Bethany, he saw a fig tree bearing no fruit and cursed it so that it withered away. Doesn't that seem contrary to his nature—to curse a tree because it had no fruit? Swedenborg explains that he wasn't looking for something to eat; he was trying to teach a lesson. The fig tree, he says, represents the state of the church, the quality of God's presence with the people. The fig tree was barren and cursed because there was nothing spiritual in it: no fruit. This was the state of the people and God's presence within them. This is why Jesus wept. And this is why the people, because they rejected him, were cursed.

The confrontation began when the priests and scribes felt their power threatened. When they saw "the amazing things that he did, and heard the children crying out in the temple, 'Hosanna to the

Son of David,' they became angry" (Matthew 21:15) and openly challenged him.

> Then the assembly rose as a body and brought Jesus before Pilate. They began to accuse him, saying, "We found this man perverting our nation, forbidding us to pay taxes to the emperor, and saying that he himself is the Messiah, a king." . . . Then Pilate said to the chief priests and the crowds, "I find no basis for an accusation against this man." But they were insistent and said, "He stirs up the people by teaching throughout all Judea, from Galilee where he began even to this place." (Luke 23:1–2, 4–5)

Yes, Jesus was stirring up the people—rousing them from their spiritual lethargy. It is something God still does to help us regenerate. Regeneration requires stirring things up within us as we endure our challenges. The process may bring up "remains"—Swedenborg's term for the experiences and feelings planted in us as babies and children that remain subconsciously with us and come to life whenever we are touched by heaven. God is present with us in those times through our own conscience, Swedenborg says, inspiring us to do what we know is right and to reflect on anything that might have hurt others.

This sets up a clash of feelings within us. We are left with a choice to either embrace heavenly love or follow a more material path. This was what was "stirred up" in the people of Jerusalem—some were willing to follow Jesus, while others were out to destroy him. Our own challenge may not be as dramatic as what led to the Crucifixion, but we are choosing all the time whether to put God first or turn away from him.

It was in the middle of that fateful week between Palm Sunday and Easter that Jesus celebrated Passover with his disciples. This ancient holy day is still observed by Jews, celebrating their deliverance from slavery in Egypt. Swedenborg says it also symbolizes our own "deliverance" from any habit or obsession that enslaves us and our eventual rebirth as spiritual people.

When Jesus was eating the Passover meal with his disciples, he set the scene for what was to come:

"Truly I tell you, one of you will betray me." And they became greatly distressed and began to say to him one after another, "Surely not I, Lord?" He answered, "The one who has dipped his hand into the bowl with me will betray me. The Son of Man goes as it is written of him, but woe to that one by whom the Son of Man is betrayed! It would have been better for that one not to have been born." Judas, who betrayed him, said, "Surely not I, Rabbi?" He replied, "You have said so." (Matthew 26:21–25)

How, we might wonder, could anyone who had faithfully followed Jesus turn and betray him? This leads to another question: Why would God allow it? Why would God allow Adam and Eve to be seduced by the serpent in the garden of Eden, allow Cain to slay Abel, allow Jesus himself to be crucified, or allow any of the unjust things we see in the Bible and in our own lives?

Swedenborg explains that it all goes back to God loving us enough to give us free will—even, and especially, the freedom to go against his will. As we saw in previous chapters, when we value our own prudence—our ability to decide for ourselves what to do in any situation—it can lead us to think that we know better than what God has commanded, that we can choose for ourselves what is best.

This is where Judas was. Whatever his motives, he was acting from his own self-centered perspective, in the most negative way imaginable, and thus became the ultimate symbol of betrayal.

It is significant that Jesus did not stop Judas from what he was about to do but instead made him think about it. At Easter, many Christians examine themselves and commit to being better people. It is also a time to recognize how God works with us. He doesn't stop us from acting against his will, but he does ask us to reflect on what we are doing. We may have something of Judas in us at times, but God never abandons us. He is always reaching out to the "better angels" within us. Indeed, he offered that hope within the celebration of Passover, just after Judas sealed his own fate. Even though Jesus knew who would betray him, he still included Judas in his invitation:

While they were eating, Jesus took a loaf of bread, and after
blessing it he broke it, gave it to the disciples, and said, "Take,
eat; this is my body." Then he took a cup, and after giving thanks
he gave it to them, saying, "Drink from it, all of you; for this is
my blood of the covenant, which is poured out for many for the
forgiveness of sins. I tell you, I will never again drink of this fruit
of the vine until that day when I drink it new with you in my
Father's kingdom." (Matthew 26:26–29)

In John, we learn that Jesus also instructed them to live lives full
of love: "I give you a new commandment, that you love one another.
Just as I have loved you, you also should love one another. By this
everyone will know that you are my disciples, if you have love for
one another" (John 13:34–35).

Even though Jesus knew the end was at hand, he was talking
about new life—the life that comes with springtime, the life that
comes to all of us when we put aside our old ways and become
"born from above," as Jesus advised Nicodemus in John 3:3.

We see the theme of life once again after the Resurrection, when
Jesus again spoke to the disciples: "He breathed on them and said to
them, 'Receive the Holy Spirit'" (John 20:22). Swedenborg writes,
"Life is renewed when a spiritual influence from the inner dimension acts on the contents of the earthly plane from within" (*Secrets
of Heaven* §5972). And breathing has a special significance:

Breathing on them was an act that represented the imparting
of life through faith and love, as was breathing into the human
in Genesis 2:7: "Jehovah breathed into [the human's] nostrils
the breath of lives, and the human was made into a living soul."
(*Secrets of Heaven* §9229:3)

God created the world and created us, and he is perpetually
breathing life into his creation. But before we can grasp this new
spirit comes the horror of Good Friday—a day that seems anything but "good"—and the Crucifixion. Why did Jesus, this good
and innocent man, have to suffer by being beaten, nailed to a cross,
and taunted? Why was he demeaned with a crown of thorns and
mocked as the "King of the Jews"?

No doubt those who abused and killed him were sure they had won and that, for all the promise Jesus brought into the world, he had been defeated. But, Swedenborg teaches, the Crucifixion was the culmination of his purpose in coming on earth. It was his crowning victory for all of us.

When the crowds screamed "Crucify him!" and the soldiers did so, Jesus did not turn away from their hatred. His love and mercy are for everyone, even those who are opposed to him. Swedenborg writes that God is pure love, and it was his mercy that led to his incarnation as Jesus:

> The pure love [that is the divine essence] is pure mercy. . . .
> That is why it came into the world and underwent temptations
> even to the final one, the suffering on the cross; it is constantly
> at work to make the unclean clean and the insane sane, so it is
> constantly laboring out of pure mercy. (*Divine Providence* §337)

Indeed, Swedenborg explains, God's willingness to undergo the most extreme temptation—not just the pain and ignominy of the Crucifixion but also the attack on what he cared about most, the salvation of the human race—is what this transforming event is all about.

It is easy to condemn those who cried out for his crucifixion, as though we would never have been a part of that. But every time we turn away from God with anger, selfishness, or lust, we become a part of that crowd. And he still loves us and offers his mercy. On Good Friday, we are asked to reflect on how quick we may be to condemn those who oppose us, on how slow we may be to show them mercy, and on what Jesus's ultimate example says to us about loving one another.

We may view God at times as judging and condemning, particularly when we read the Old Testament, but Swedenborg assures us that God never judges or condemns. As human beings, we are sometimes inclined to judge others, and so we may see God that way. Swedenborg portrays God as always loving, supporting, and leading us, never angry or punishing. We are the ones who may turn away, abandon him, and judge others. And so, he warns, we may be the ones judging—or misjudging—God, not the other way around.

From these few points you can see how insane people are who think that God can condemn anyone, curse anyone, throw anyone into hell, predestine anyone's soul to eternal death, avenge wrongs, or rage against or punish anyone. People are even more insane if they actually believe this, let alone teach it. In reality, God cannot turn away from us or even look at us with a frown. To do any such thing would be against his essence, and what is against his essence is against himself. (*True Christianity* §56)

Even in his last hours of despair on the cross—and in the events that happened immediately after his death—Jesus still was teaching. In the Gospel of Matthew (27:45–53), it describes how darkness covered the earth in the last three hours of his crucifixion. Finally, he cried out with a loud voice and gave up the spirit. Then everything turned cataclysmic, with earthquakes and fire, graves splitting open, and the bodies of saints flowing out into the city. It must have been a terrifying scene for anyone who witnessed it.

But all of this chaos, Swedenborg explains, represented why God came on earth and what he accomplished with both his life and his death. "The curtain [or veil] of the temple," for example, had always been a barrier between the people and God. Behind it was the Word of God and a brilliant light, but only the high priest was allowed inside. The people on the other side of the veil were in twilight, unable to see clearly. Once the curtain "was torn in two, from top to bottom" (Matthew 27:51), the light went out to the people and they could finally see and know God. That, Swedenborg says, is what Jesus's life and death accomplished for us.

Out of the sadness and despair of the Crucifixion comes the triumph of Easter and its promise. We see Mary Magdalene and "Mary the mother of James and Joseph" (Matthew 27:56) come to the tomb to care for Jesus's body, only to find the stone rolled away. How devastated they must have felt to find the tomb empty. But an angel quickly told them not to be afraid, for "he has been raised" (Matthew 28:7). Then they ran to tell the good news to the disciples.

Recall from earlier in this chapter that God's purpose in coming to earth as Jesus was to cause a spiritual transformation not only in our world but also in the next. The Crucifixion and the Resurrection are the culmination of that battle.

> If you knew what hell is like, and you knew how high it swelled and how it flooded the entire world of spirits at the time of the Lord's coming, and you saw the great power with which the Lord cast hell down and scattered it and then restructured both it and heaven in accordance with the divine design, you could not help being stunned and exclaiming that all of it was something only the Divine could do....
>
> The Lord's battle with hell can also be compared, although inadequately, with someone fighting against all the wild animals in the world, slaughtering or taming them until not one animal would dare to go out and attack any human being who is with the Lord. (*True Christianity* §123:1, 4)

God's mission on earth was completed with his resurrection, Swedenborg says, but Jesus did not ascend into heaven immediately. He still had lessons to teach.

Imagine how the disciples felt after the man they hailed as their Lord and savior was crucified before their eyes. They had not stood up for him. They had abandoned him. When Jesus predicted Peter would deny him three times, Peter glibly proclaimed that he would never do so—and later wept bitterly when he realized how easily he had betrayed his own word.

When Jesus appeared to them after his resurrection, they must have been afraid. Maybe they thought they were seeing a ghost. Once they accepted what had happened, they probably expected him to be angry. But his first words to them—as recorded in Luke—were, "Peace be with you" (24:36). He showed them his true nature: love and forgiveness, compassion and mercy.

Before he came to earth, God's presence with people was indirect and perhaps more easily ignored. Once he came and lived and taught among the people, Swedenborg says, his presence became direct, so that now we can know him and form a relationship with him.

The happy ending that followed the horror of the Crucifixion is celebrated at Easter but is with us every day, just as is the Christmas story of God being born within us. God did not leave his disciples, the women who loved him, and other followers destitute with grief. Before he rose into heaven, he came back to them, to reassure them and help them understand. It was his loving presence that took away their fear and doubts—his promise that "I am with you always, to the end of the age" (Matthew 28:20).

We can get much of this from the plain telling of the Bible, but Swedenborg shows how the internal sense enhances the meaning of it all for our lives. This internal sense, he says, is God coming again as he promised—as the "Spirit of truth [who] will guide you into all the truth" (John 16:13).

In spite of everything that confronts us in our lives, God still says to us, "Take courage; I have conquered the world" (John 16:33). His gift to us, Swedenborg explains, was simply coming on earth and becoming visible to us, and we can see that most clearly in the Christmas and Easter stories. For those who believe, these stories serve as encouragement to make room for God in the "inn" of our minds, to learn from the parables and teachings of his life, and to learn from our spiritual trials—the Good Fridays of life—to experience the joyful deliverance of Easter.

He is risen that we may be also.

8

THE BOOK OF REVELATION
A "BRIGHT MORNING STAR"

The book of Revelation is written largely in symbols.
— Joseph Franklin Rutherford

The Bible is a revelation of the mind and will of God to men.
Therein we may learn, what God is.
— Jupiter Hammon

A true servant of God will never teach a false doctrine. He will
never deny new revelation. He will never tell you that the canon
of scripture is full, or that the New Testament is the last revelation ever intended to be given to man.
— Orson Pratt

The Bible, as a revelation from God, was not designed to give
us all the information we might desire, nor to solve all the questions about which the human soul is perplexed, but to impart
enough to be a safeguard to the haven of eternal rest.
— Albert Barnes

Dan Brown's 2009 bestseller *The Lost Symbol* is a search for a key to unlock the inner meaning of the Bible. Emanuel Swedenborg claims to have been given that key. And nowhere is the symbolism of the Bible more important, enigmatic, inscrutable, and in need of a key than it is in the book of Revelation.

Many scholars consider it an unfathomable mystery, perhaps not even meant to be understood. Unlike the simple stories in the rest of the Bible, Revelation is more like an abstract painting, inviting interpretation but defying consensus. Amid a maze of visions and symbols, Revelation reads like prophecy, as though something significant is going to happen. Because so many of its images are filled with foreboding—seven-headed beasts, stars falling from heaven, a darkened sun and moon, heaven and earth passing away—end-of-the-world scenarios are inevitable.

But if this concluding book of the Bible is never meant to be understood, why is it even there? Many Christians believe it must also contain God's truth to teach and guide our lives. But whatever meanings are hidden there, Revelation's spiritual message is even more obscure than those of the rest of the Bible. Swedenborg insists that John's visions on the Isle of Patmos—like Swedenborg's own visions—were not the product of his own imagination but that he saw what he saw for a reason. Indeed, Revelation opens with the steadfast declaration that the text is "the revelation of Jesus Christ, which God gave him to show his servants what must soon take place; he made it known by sending his angel to his servant John" (Revelation 1:1).

Even though John was still in this world, Swedenborg says, what he saw was actually occurring in the spiritual world. What is really going on in Revelation, Swedenborg teaches, is a spiritual judgment that ends with God re-establishing his kingdom on earth. Rather than describing an end-of-the-world cataclysm, Swedenborg's interpretation offers a triumphant message of love and hope.

Many Christians have interpreted Revelation as a prophecy of the Last Judgment—a final, cataclysmic event playing out on earth that will culminate with God returning here to live and rule. Some believers may have been left wondering as predictions of an end-of-the-world apocalypse and rapture have come and gone. Swedenborg explains that what is portrayed in Revelation is real, but the biblical book actually describes the judgment of the world and the spiritual state of its people. In fact, he claims to have witnessed this judgment in the spiritual world in the year 1757. Swedenborg describes a process of sorting good people from evil that restored order between heaven and hell, thereby restoring spiritual freedom to the human race so that we are free to choose between good and evil, heaven and hell.

The dramatic images in Revelation can be dark and scary, but the root meaning of *apocalypse* is to uncover or reveal. This is what Swedenborg offers: a revelation, or uncovering, from God. In fact, Revelation concludes not with the end of the world but with a peaceful and inspiring vision of "a new heaven and a new earth."

Swedenborg also teaches that God's second coming is entirely different from his first. This is not God coming back to earth again as Jesus, he says, and is not the violent upheaval portrayed in the literal words of Revelation. Yes, there is a pitched battle between good and evil in the spiritual world, followed by a "second coming" that is peaceful, spiritual, and real. This, he explains, is the promised "Spirit of truth" come to "guide you into all the truth" (John 16:13). What it means, he says, is that God is coming personally to each of us, making it possible to see him as a visible God and approach him in the Bible with new understanding and appreciation.

What is most significant about this Last Judgment and second coming, Swedenborg teaches, is that these events—two hundred and fifty years ago and in a spiritual realm far removed from our experience—offer us a new, personal relationship with God. He stands at the door of our lives, Swedenborg says, knocking and waiting to be received.

> Few today know what the Last Judgment is. Most think it will come with the end of the world. As a result, they speculate that the whole inhabited world, along with everything visible in it, will be destroyed by fire. The dead will then rise for the first time and be presented for judgment, they believe, and bad people will be thrown into hell, while good people will go up into heaven.
>
> These theories come from scriptural prophecies that mention a new sky and earth and a new Jerusalem as well. The theorizers do not realize that the meaning of scriptural prophecies in an inner sense differs radically from their evident meaning in the literal sense. They fail to see that *the sky* does not mean the sky, or *the earth*, the earth, but the Lord's church as a whole and as it exists with every individual in particular. (*Secrets of Heaven* §2117)

One of the ways in which the inner and literal senses are radically different, he says, is that the judgment was being made on the church of his day. This refers not just to institutions or denominations but to the quality of personal faith—the "church" that exists within people. So the Last Judgment means something for each of us as well, just as everything in the Bible relates directly to our lives. The judgment presented in Revelation, he says, is both broad (the state of the church as a whole) and intensely personal (the state of our own spiritual life).

But while the prospect of being judged can be intimidating, Swedenborg assures us that anyone who has led a good life has nothing to fear. The new heaven proclaimed in Revelation has twelve gates, not just one. This illustrates that there are many ways to enter heaven and that no one who loves God and lives according to his commandments will be kept out.

Swedenborg explains that the twelve gates, each formed from one pearl, stand for the different ways that knowing goodness and truth lead people to a new understanding of the Divine—the "New Jerusalem" that marks a new spiritual age for humanity. The fact that these gates "will never be shut by day—and there will be no night there" (Revelation 21:25) means that the light of truth is always there to lead us and that there is nothing false there.

But what happens with those who believe they should be admitted to heaven but who don't really belong? If people who don't live lives of goodness and truth try to enter, "they are not received because they do not fit in, and they then either leave of their own accord, since they cannot stand the light there, or they are sent away" (*Revelation Unveiled* §922).

These twelve gates are similar to what John refers to in his letter to the Church of Philadelphia earlier in Revelation: "Look, I have set before you an open door, which no one is able to shut" (Revelation 3:8).

One of the visions Swedenborg describes is of a magnificent temple that represents the new church—the New Jerusalem, or new understanding—established in heaven with the Last Judgment. Inscribed above the entrance are the words *Nunc Licet*, meaning *Now It Is Allowed*. Swedenborg says he was told by angels that this meant people would be able now to explore and understand the spiritual meanings of the Bible (*True Christianity* §508:3). The temple is a symbol of a new church being established in heaven and on earth—and in the minds of all those who come to see and understand the internal, spiritual meaning of the Bible.

So now let us enter into the mysteries of the book of Revelation.

Seven Churches

In the Gospel of John, Jesus says that John would not die until he had come again (21:23). It is thought to be sixty years after the Crucifixion when John was exiled to the Isle of Patmos in the Aegean Sea. But it was there that God opened John's eyes to the visions he was told to write down for the seven churches in Asia Minor. This is considered by some to be the beginning of the Christian church, based on the vision of a living God.

After the opening declaration that everything in this book is "the revelation of Jesus Christ," John is instructed to write to the seven churches of Asia: Ephesus, Smyrna, Pergamum, Thyatira, Sardis, Philadelphia, and Laodicea. The names of the churches, Swedenborg says, represent spiritual qualities. In the spiritual sense, these are not specific, established churches; rather, they represent the different ways that people see and respond to God. This is the "church" within us—our personal faith.

For each of these churches, God's message begins with "I know your works." These "works" a term that refers to the ways in which the members of the church put their beliefs into action—may have either a positive or negative connotation, but they all speak to some quality of faith within each of us.

- The *church of Ephesus* represents people who are so focused on doctrinal truths that they forget to apply those good teachings to their lives.

- The *church of Smyrna* represents people who strive to do good works throughout their lives but have the wrong idea about what is true.

- The *church of Pergamum* represents people who likewise always strive to do good works; while they understand spiritual truths, they believe the truth is irrelevant as long as they do good works.

- The *church of Thyatira* represents two different types of people: On the positive end of the scale are those who do good works out of a genuine love for all people (in the older, broader sense of the word *charity*). On the negative end are people who likewise do good in the world but who are motivated by selfish goals like improving their reputation. Swedenborg tells us that no matter what good those self-centered people do, when it's not motivated by love, the result is nothing but evil.

- The *church of Sardis* represents those who are in the worst state of all; they neither do good works nor believe in spiritual truths, and therefore there is no life in their worship.

- The *church of Philadelphia* represents the opposite: people who live good lives out of a genuine love for others and also believe in spiritual truth.

- The *church of Laodicea* represents people who are "neither cold nor hot" (Revelation 3:16) because their rationality is always fighting against their faith; they choose to believe only some of the spiritual truths that they've learned, and by putting their trust in themselves rather than in God, they've distanced themselves from the Divine.

All of the book of Revelation, Swedenborg says, is addressed to these "churches"—which in this case represent the particular quality of faith within each of us. The letters to the churches are calling on us to pay attention to our inner state and showing us how to grow spiritually.

These churches also represent all people who have religion in their lives and from whom a broader new church—the new spiritual age known as the New Jerusalem—can be formed. But we are cautioned: "Let anyone who has an ear listen to what the Spirit is saying to the churches" (Revelation 2:7). We need to pay attention to what this means in our lives, Swedenborg says, because the message that courses through the images and visions of Revelation is all about judgment and deliverance. It's a judgment on the state of the "church," which means on the state of our own spiritual condition. Churches are judged by how true they are to God's teachings. Similarly, he says, we are judged by the choices we make throughout our lives, and the path we choose to walk will define our life after death.

In the letter to the church of Ephesus, John records this message from God: "Remember then from what you have fallen; repent, and do the works you did at first. If not, I will come to you and remove your lampstand from its place, unless you repent." And he adds: "To everyone who conquers, I will give permission to eat from the tree of life that is in the paradise of God" (Revelation 2:5, 7).

Swedenborg explains that when we put the truth first in our lives, we are like promising but unripe fruit. We become "ripe" through regeneration—shunning evil and living God's teachings. He tells of seeing people in the spiritual world turned toward either heaven or hell by how they viewed truth. This quality of life, he says in *Revelation Unveiled* §84, "is accomplished by repenting and then, after that, by living in such a way as to do good," which is what is meant by "repent, and do the works you did at first" (Revelation 2:5).

Each image in these letters holds a spiritual meaning, Swedenborg tells us. For example, the lampstand stands for enlightenment, and it is to be removed if the church does not regenerate. Removing it means that truth cannot be seen in its own light; rather, it can only be seen through spiritual understanding from God, who is the only real source of enlightenment.

To everyone who conquers means those who fight against evil and falsity and therefore can be reformed.

I will give permission to eat from the tree of life. It is significant that the tree of life appears in the very first chapter of Genesis and in the very last chapter of Revelation. In both cases, it is a symbol of all the goodness and love within God. *To eat* means to make something our own. So eating of the fruit of the tree of life brings God's love into our lives. As earthly fruit sustains our bodies, spiritual fruit sustains our souls and helps us to lead lives of kindness.

Swedenborg says it is also significant that John's letters are sent to seven churches, and he points out that the number seven is repeated throughout Revelation. John's first vision is of seven golden lampstands and seven stars in the hand of the Son of Man.

Throughout the book, we see references to seven seals, seven kings, seven trumpets, a seven-headed dragon, seven bowls, seven plagues, and seven angels.

Remember that Swedenborg says everything in the Bible— every word, every name, every number—has a correspondence that helps us understand the spiritual sense.

> Numbers in the Word have substantive meaning, and seven
> means all things and all people. It therefore also means whatever
> is full and complete; and it is used in the Word in connection
> with what is holy, and in its opposite sense with what is unholy.
> (*Revelation Unveiled* §10)

Four Horses and Seven Seals

John's next vision is of the throne of God in heaven, surrounded by a rainbow and twenty-four elders with white robes and golden crowns. Lightning and thunder come out of the throne, which is surrounded by seven lamps of fire and four beasts—a lion, a calf, a man, and an eagle. Revelation 4 ends with: "You are worthy, our Lord and God, to receive glory and honor and power, for you created all things, and by your will they existed and were created" (11).

All of this, Swedenborg writes, is about heaven being prepared for the judgment to come and about acknowledging that God is the only judge. Each of the strange beasts represents a different type of divine understanding, which is the only way to truly perceive the difference between right and wrong. Brought down into our own lives, he says, this vision is about God's power to give us the understanding, wisdom, and ability to do what is good so that we can come into heaven.

Then comes the vision of a book sealed with seven seals, which only the Lamb is worthy to open. Swedenborg explains that the Lamb represents God, risen from his crucifixion to judge the falsities in the church—and in our hearts—and lead us to heaven. "Worthy is the Lamb that was slaughtered to receive power and wealth and wisdom and might and honor and glory and blessing" (Revelation 5:12).

When the first four seals are opened, four horsemen ride out on white, red, black, and pale horses. The white horse is said to represent a true understanding of God's Word; the red horse, an understanding stained by selfish love; the black horse, ignorance, or no understanding at all; and the pale horse, an understanding that has been destroyed or profaned and is therefore a threat to the faith of others.

When the fifth seal is opened, souls are seen under the altar. Swedenborg says that these souls are the people who had upheld divine truths even when it meant being rejected by others around them; now, in this time of turbulence and judgment, God is protecting them.

With the opening of the sixth seal, there is a great earthquake; the sun becomes black and the moon as red as blood. This frightening imagery represents what God sees when he begins to examine the inner state of evil people in the spiritual world: the total rejection of love, truth, and goodness. For our own lives, this is a warning to those who walk in darkness. While in this world, even those who have made mistakes or been in places where they reject love because of doubt or pain can turn their lives around if they choose to do so.

In the midst of the turbulence following the opening of the sixth seal, John describes angels holding back the destruction of the land so that God can separate out the ones who have held goodness and truth in their hearts. We are given the very specific number of one hundred and forty-four thousand. Some Christians have taken this quite literally, believing that this represents an exact number of elect people who will be allowed into heaven and that all others will be shut out. It is understandable to draw such a conclusion from the literal words alone, but it flies in the face of what Swedenborg teaches us about God: that he loves everyone, constantly tries to raise us to heaven, and withholds salvation from no one.

Swedenborg tells us that the number one hundred and forty-four thousand "signifies all who acknowledge the Lord to be the God of heaven and earth" and who live good lives of love and truth (*Apocalypse Revealed* §348). The number derives from twelve thousand people from each of the twelve tribes of Israel, who represent the church—that is, the group of believers—created from the good and the faithful. The number twelve here means all, in its simplest form. Swedenborg adds that in this case, it also represents the New Jerusalem—the church that is to come, created from the good people of the previous age. Thus the number given does not literally refer to a specific number of people; it is all of the good people in the world, regardless of the number.

We are told, "These are they who have come out of the great ordeal; they have washed their robes and made them white in the blood of the Lamb" (Revelation 7:14). There is no way that robes literally can be washed in blood to make them white, but Swedenborg explains that blood represents truth. We are purified through the spiritual washing of regeneration, he says—by God's truth.

Then comes the comforting promise: "The Lamb at the center of the throne will be their shepherd, and he will guide them to springs of the water of life, and God will wipe away every tear from their eyes" (Revelation 7:17). The people of this new spiritual age will no longer experience the trials and tribulations of before; there is nothing before them but heavenly joy.

When the seventh seal is opened there is complete silence in heaven. Swedenborg tells us that this signifies the angels' amazement at the state of faith in spiritual people.

Seven Angels and Seven Trumpets

Seven angels blow seven trumpets, heralding something new and holy for the world. But Swedenborg says that anyone who lives by faith alone—believing that faith is all that matters, not the way we live our lives—is deaf to the trumpets. So they suffered plagues of fire and blood, a third of the creatures in the sea died, the sun and the moon and the stars were dimmed, and there was a plague of locusts that lasted five months—all of these things representing the corruption of a church with no love in it.

Before the seventh angel sounds his trumpet, he gives a little book to John and commands him to eat it, saying it will be sweet as honey in his mouth but bitter in his belly. This book, Swedenborg explains, is the doctrine of the new church that the Lord God Jesus Christ is establishing in heaven and on earth. All of this, he says, can seem sweet to the tongue—or ear. But when we take the teachings into our lives and try to live by them, they may be hard to stomach if we don't fully accept them.

John was told to keep trying: "You must prophesy again about many peoples and nations and languages and kings" (Revelation 10:11). The message ultimately is hopeful. It says that we can do this and that it is what God wants from us.

Swedenborg says that the two witnesses sent to guide the journey—two olive trees and two lampstands—represent love and intelligence, or faith and charity, the pillars of God's new revelation. They have great power but are opposed by people whose mistaken view of worship seeks to destroy them, represented by the beasts rising out of the bottomless pit. When the beasts kill them, their bodies lie in the street for three-and-a-half days, rotting and scorned, their enemies rejoicing over them. But then the Spirit of God enters into their bodies and they are revived and called up into heaven. Just imagine the fear then of those who had mocked them. Swedenborg says this shows how God takes care of and provides for everyone who follows him—no matter what forces are arrayed against us.

Finally, that seventh trumpet sounds and there is great rejoicing in heaven for the re-establishment of God's kingdom. But it is accompanied by "flashes of lightning, rumblings, peals of thunder, an earthquake, and heavy hail" (Revelation 11:19), signifying that there were still people who didn't want to let go of their old beliefs in the lower parts of the spiritual world.

The Dragon and the Woman Clothed with the Sun

There is foreboding in all of this. What follows is the promising image of the woman clothed with the sun, with the moon under her feet and a crown of twelve stars, crying out in pain as she prepares to deliver her child. But before her stands a menacing red dragon with seven heads, seven crowns, and ten horns, ready to devour her child as soon as it is born.

Revelation 12:1–9 describe how the woman brings forth "a male child, who is to rule all the nations with a rod of iron." Her baby is then "snatched away and taken to God and to his throne," while she is driven into the wilderness to escape the dragon in a place prepared by God. A great war in heaven ensues, with Michael and his angels slaying the dragon.

The woman clothed with the sun, Swedenborg teaches, is a symbol of spiritual truth giving birth to the heavenly doctrines that are establishing a new church in heaven and on earth. This is the power of God's truth come to rule in our minds, he says—if we accept it.

That church becomes possible, he explains, as the falsities of the existing church are exposed. The child represents new doctrine from God. The dragon is the threat to this new understanding of faith. Michael and his angels are those who believe in one God and live by the Ten Commandments. The dragons they slay are those who believe that faith is all that matters, not the quality of our lives.

This part of the story is a promising deliverance from all the sadness and challenges that came with the seven seals and the seven trumpets. But there will always be dragons. Even those who sincerely love God and try to live good lives, Swedenborg says, will have their faith attacked. Even when the dragon is cast out of heaven by Michael and his angels, it still persecutes the woman, but she is given the wings of an eagle to fly into the wilderness, where she is nourished and protected "for a time, and times, and half a time" (Revelation 12:14).

Swedenborg says that the curious phrase "a time, and times, and half a time" means "the end of the former church and the beginning of the new"—the beginning of the new church in heaven and on earth (*Apocalypse Revealed* §547).

Still attempting to kill the woman, the dragon spews a flood of water out of its mouth, threatening to drown people with endless appeals to selfishness. But the earth swallows up the flood, signifying that the truth can always absorb and overcome false reasoning.

Like the woman, we are never completely safe in this world, and this is because of our freedom. God grants us the freedom to choose between good and evil, and Swedenborg teaches that we must be exposed to evil so that we can really know what it is before we can choose what is good. Then—and only then—can we be safe from the dragons.

The foiled dragon was angry and "went off to make war on the rest of her children, those who keep the commandments of God and hold the testimony of Jesus" (Revelation 12:17).

No sooner is one dragon subdued than another rises out of the sea—this one like a leopard, with the feet of a bear and the mouth of a lion, seven heads and ten horns, "and on its heads were blasphemous names" (Revelation 13:1). And another beast also rises out of the earth, deceiving people with illusions. This is the beast with the infamous 666, and anyone who bears this mark is doomed.

Swedenborg explains that the number six corresponds to what is holy and complete but that every correspondence also has an opposite meaning. Water, for instance, stands for truth, but with Noah and the Flood, water represents the drowning tide of evil and falsity. In this case, he says, 666 stands for the falsification and corruption of the Bible. This is the beast who wants to be worshipped as a false God. Its attacks are subtle and beguiling, like the voice that says it's OK to break a commandment if it doesn't hurt anyone and feels good.

The relentlessness of these dragons—making people doubt or become susceptible to acting against what they say they believe—was brilliantly captured by C. S. Lewis in his classic book titled *The Screwtape Letters*. This is a collection of scurrilous letters from Screwtape, a highly placed assistant to "Our Father Below," to his nephew and novice demon, Wormwood. Screwtape is mentoring Wormwood on how to corrupt the soul of an unsuspecting and well-inclined young man and secure his damnation. The implication is that the process can be that subtle and insidious for any of us—unaware of the dragons (or Wormwoods) preying on us.

It is no coincidence that the apprentice devil trying out his evil wiles on the innocent young man is named Wormwood. The name comes from Revelation 8:11, as the angels are sounding their trumpets and a star falls from the sky: "The name of the star is Wormwood. A third of the waters became wormwood, and many died from the water, because it was made bitter."

Swedenborg says that the star, in this case, represents our own pride of self-intelligence and that its name signifies the way our intelligence can be corrupted by falsifying the truths of the Bible, making them say what we want them to say.

This book by Lewis is a favorite of many Christians for the way it portrays the temptations we all must deal with and how we can triumph over them. In one of his letters, the devious Screwtape advises Wormwood:

> Do remember, the only thing that matters is the extent to which you separate the man from the Enemy. [The Enemy, of course, is God and heaven.] It does not matter how small the sins are provided that their cumulative effect is to edge the man away from the Light and into the Nothing. Murder is no better than cards if cards can do the trick. Indeed the safest road to Hell is the gradual one—the gentle slope, soft underfoot, without sudden turnings, without milestones, without signposts. (Lewis 2001, 60)

Screwtape, Wormwood, dragons—they are always after us, trying to turn us toward the darkness. The hope given to us in Revelation is that God is always with us and that Michael and his angels are ready to help slay the dragons if that protection is what we choose.

Throughout Revelation, this free choice is portrayed as two sides in an enduring conflict within our own minds—between heaven and hell, good and evil, God and the devil.

Babylon and the Plagues

Next in the account, we see the Lamb again—always representing God—standing on Mount Zion with those one hundred and forty-four thousand souls singing "a new song," because they have chosen God and have "[the Lamb's] name and his Father's name written on their foreheads" (Revelation 14:1). They represent all people who have been redeemed and rejoice because of their faith and good lives. Still they are warned by the angels not to worship the beast or to wear his mark but instead to "fear God and give him glory, for the hour of his judgment has come" (Revelation 14:7).

Then another angel proclaims, "Fallen, fallen is Babylon the great! She has made all nations drink of the wine of the wrath of her fornication" (Revelation 14:8).

Babylon is mentioned throughout the Bible, always with a negative connotation. Swedenborg says Babylon represents lust for power, control, and dominion. The woman associated with Babylon in Revelation, he adds, represents the desire to control others, with the power to claim their souls and decide whether they will go to heaven or hell.

Babylon also stands as a warning about what happens when power becomes all that is important and corrupts a church. It is a threat within us, too, he says, when our own craving for power and control turns us away from God and the life that leads to love, peace, and happiness. When people ignore or distort the teachings of the Bible by not keeping the Ten Commandments and not living a life of charity, all that is left of their "church" is the corrupting love of power, dominion, and control.

Swedenborg warns that this is one of the toughest challenges we face:

> The hardest battle of all, though, is with our love of being in control because of our sense of self-importance. If we overcome this, we have no trouble overcoming our other evil loves, because this is the head of them all. (*Divine Providence* §146)

The opposite of this love of dominion is a noble love of ruling. This is a love of serving by leading people to good and loving lives. God himself is the ultimate good "ruler," which is why he is always represented by the Lamb of innocence.

Another angel in John's vision has a sharp sickle, gathering in "the clusters of the vine of the earth"—the grapes of wrath (Revelation 14:18). This represents people who choose to be worldly and selfish, instead of loving God and their neighbor, and the process of being pressed into wine represents God's process of examining their inner selves. They suffer the "wrath" they bring on themselves by clinging to false beliefs.

All of this, Swedenborg teaches, is precursor to God's Last Judgment upon the fallen church. It is played out in the scene from Revelation 16 in which seven angels pour out the seven last plagues on the earth from seven bowls. As each is poured out, the judgment is completed. These include water turning into blood, men scorched with fire, ominous darkness, terrible sores, and frogs coming out of the mouth of the dragon. Swedenborg tells us that the contents of the bowls represent divine love flowing in from God—it only becomes something horrible when it pours into people who are clinging to self-serving beliefs and attitudes. This is how John's vision plays out in our own lives every day, Swedenborg warns. Good intentions can turn to horrible results when we act out of self-love rather than out of love toward others.

The plagues are followed by "the great whore" seated on a scarlet beast with seven heads and ten horns, with a golden cup in her hand "full of abominations and the impurities of her fornication" (Revelation 17:1, 4). This is another representation of Babylon—of people who use selfish and worldly loves to pervert the good and truth of the Bible and to control and corrupt the lives of others.

Another angel cries with a strong voice, "Fallen, fallen is Babylon the great! It has become a dwelling place of demons, a haunt of every foul spirit, a haunt of every foul bird, a haunt of every foul and hateful beast" (Revelation 18:2). Babylon and the dragon are the enemies of a spiritual life, destroying the doctrine of the church (truth) and of life (good). As a city, Swedenborg says, Babylon represents a church—a body of believers—whose worship is based on a misinterpretation or even a deliberate twisting of divine truth. However, it can also be seen as a false system of belief that we hold individually, even with the best of intentions, which has led us into a view of the world that makes it impossible to grow closer to God.

When we come to reject the allures of Babylon, and all that it represents is "fallen" in our own lives—through the process of regeneration—we can rejoice with the angels in celebrating its fall within us.

As we are "reborn" through the process of regeneration, our lives turn toward heaven and become ever more peaceful. At this point, the tone of Revelation changes, too.

New Jerusalem

So far, John's visions have been scary and disturbing—grim warnings of spiritual dangers that we all face. Now they turn upbeat and inspiring: a white horse, the marriage of the Lamb, the dragon bound for a thousand years, and the holy city—the new Jerusalem—descending from God out of heaven. This is what happens when falsity and misunderstanding are exposed, Swedenborg teaches—when evil is seen and rejected and when God and heaven are embraced.

On the white horse is the man called "Faithful and True," who is God himself, coming as "King of kings and Lord of lords" (Revelation 19:11, 16). Here he represents not only the ruler of all creation but also God in his aspect of the love and truth coming through sacred scripture, which can now be properly understood by all.

The dragon of evil is chained and thrown into a lake of fire and brimstone, never to deceive the church again. This, also, is part of the process of regeneration: separating out the convictions that have held us back and rejecting them so that they no longer have any influence over us.

This part of Revelation also speaks of another judgment, that of the opening of each person's book of life:

> And I saw the dead, great and small, standing before the throne, and books were opened. Also another book was opened, the book of life. And the dead were judged according to their works, as recorded in the books. (20:12)

The specter of being exposed in our personal "book of life" after death, and then being judged for everything we have done, is a scary proposition. But Swedenborg assures us that we are not judged by

God and his angels; rather, we judge ourselves, in effect, through what we chose to love. If we truly love the things of heaven, there we will find our home. But if we reject God and heaven, we could never be happy there. Indeed, Swedenborg describes such people being allowed into heaven because they claim to deserve it as only finding it insufferable. They become desperate to flee to the "home" they truly love.

What comes after the judgment—once the power of evil has been removed—is the descent of a new heaven, a new earth, a new church.

> Then I saw a new heaven and a new earth; for the first heaven
> and the first earth had passed away. . . . And I saw the holy city,
> the new Jerusalem, coming down out of heaven from God, pre-
> pared as a bride adorned for her husband. (Revelation 21:1, 2)

In this instance, Swedenborg says, the bride represents the church, now "adorned" by a new understanding of spiritual truths through sacred scripture and prepared to be joined with God. But on a personal level, we can also think of the bride as a new, fuller love of God, made possible now that we can know him as a visible God.

A wonderful promise is made in this chapter of Revelation. After all of the battles with evil and dragons,

> [God] will wipe every tear from their eyes. Death will be no
> more; mourning and crying and pain will be no more, for the
> first things have passed away. And the one who was seated on the
> throne said, "See, I am making all things new." (21:4–5)

This is the culmination, Swedenborg teaches. God makes heaven new. He makes the church new. He can make us new, too, with a new spiritual understanding to guide us.

The holy city is pure gold, representing God's pure love. Its twelve gates of pearl illustrate that there is not just one way to know and live the truth and that everyone who loves God, keeps his commandments, and lives a good life can come into heaven. "And the city has no need of sun or moon to shine on it, for the glory of God is its light, and its lamp is the Lamb" (Revelation 21:23). This light, he says, is God's incandescent truth within the Bible, illuminated in the newly revealed spiritual sense.

The last chapter of Revelation (22) opens with a pure river of the water of life coming out of the throne of God and the Lamb. This is a river of spiritual enlightenment, Swedenborg teaches—a new church being established and flowing into all who receive it.

Beside the river, bearing twelve kinds of fruit, is the tree of life, "producing its fruit each month; and the leaves of the tree are for the healing of the nations" (Revelation 22:2). The promise here, Swedenborg says, is that the tree of life and its leaves are divine love; as knowledge of this love grows and spreads, it will heal us of our sins.

The new church is being established in heaven and descending to earth, he explains, as people learn and love new truth. The promise is always rooted in our freedom to accept or reject. There are "New Churches"—churches based on Swedenborg's writings—throughout the world devoted to these new teachings. They are not focused on Swedenborg himself, who called himself merely a servant of God, but on the "Spirit of truth" given through him. However, the new church proclaimed in Revelation, he assures us, is within all people, of any religion, who love and live whatever they understand of spiritual truth.

We all need to look inside ourselves at times, he says, and ponder where we are in the midst of these visions: overwhelmed by the dragon; perhaps following the siren voices of Babylon, with no love or understanding of God; or fighting with Michael and his angels to drive the dragon out so that we can be with God. Revelation is not just an account of what happened with John on the Isle of Patmos a long time ago, Swedenborg teaches. It is a prophecy given for the people of today.

This has been a summary of the highlights of the internal spiritual meaning of the book of Revelation. If you want to dig further into this interpretation, Swedenborg's two volumes of *Apocalypse*

Revealed (also translated *Revelation Unveiled*) and six volumes of *Apocalypse Explained* (also translated *Revelation Explained*) systematically explain the symbolism of the book of Revelation verse by verse, addressing every detail of John's visions.

Revelation begins with a promise: "After this I looked, and there in heaven a door stood open" (Revelation 4:1). It ends with an even fuller promise of eternal blessing:

> "It is I, Jesus, who sent my angel to you with this testimony for the churches. I am the root and the descendant of David, the bright morning star." The Spirit and the bride say, "Come." And let everyone who hears say, "Come." And let everyone who is thirsty come. Let anyone who wishes take the water of life as a gift. (22:16–17)

The whole purpose of the "second coming" in Revelation, Swedenborg teaches, is to take away our blindness by shining a new light of truth so that we can see for ourselves and freely decide what kind of spiritual life we will lead. Revelation invites us to be made new by the light of the morning star and the water of life. Then, Swedenborg assures us, we may all be like "the people who walked in darkness [who] have seen a great light" (Isaiah 9:2)—ready to be transformed.

CONCLUSION: THE GIFT

It is a mistake to look to the Bible to close a discussion; the Bible seeks to open one.

— William Sloane Coffin

Our lives are filled with gifts from God.

Every day is a gift, to use as we see fit.

Every beauty in nature is a gift.

Every loved one, every friend, is a gift.

But some of God's gifts go right to the soul.

When God came into the world, living among us as Jesus Christ, teaching the people, and letting them come to know him—that was a transcendent gift.

The Bible is also a gift. For those who read it as sacred scripture, it is where God dwells and speaks to those who follow him. It is full of his presence and his love. As Swedenborg puts it:

> The Word is like a case that has precious stones, pearls, and gems laid out in a pattern inside. When we regard the Word as holy and read it in order to have a useful life, our minds have thoughts like a jewel case that someone takes hold of and sends up to heaven. (*True Christianity* §238)

Many of those who read and love the Bible say that they see divinity within it, even if they don't understand it completely. But fewer people seem to be growing up with the Bible, as many have come to see it as just a collection of stories from long ago that is irrelevant to their lives. Swedenborg recognizes that it is indeed easy for such people to disregard and even scorn the Bible, when they see all the violence and cruelty and wonder: Where is God in all of this? Where is the holiness? Can this really be divine? How could a loving God really speak and act like this? (See *Sacred Scripture* §1.)

2 Kings 22 tells of the high priest Hilkiah exclaiming, "I have found the book of the law in the house of the Lord" (8). The book had been put away and forgotten, but once King Josiah heard the words of the book of the law, he realized that "great is the wrath of the Lord that is kindled against us, because our ancestors did not obey the words of this book" (13). He set about changing his ways and the ways of his kingdom, and he was spared by God.

How easy it is for us also to "lose" the Bible, "the book of the law"—to let it sit forgotten on a bookshelf or in our minds. Swedenborg says it can become a greater part of our lives when we look more deeply into what it is saying. He recognizes that the Bible is difficult enough to understand even in the literal sense, and to look beyond that takes real study.

God did not give us the Bible to chastise us or make us feel bad. He gave it to inspire and save us. Swedenborg assures us that if we read it with a humble and affirmative sense that it is God speaking to us, we may become like the disciples of Jesus: not understanding everything but still seeing clearly enough to be led by God.

The Second Epistle of Paul the Apostle to the Corinthians describes how this works:

> Such is the confidence that we have through Christ toward God.
> Not that we are competent of ourselves to claim anything as coming from us; our competence is from God, who has made us competent to be ministers of a new covenant, not of letter but of spirit; *for the letter kills, but the Spirit gives life.* (3:4–6; emphasis added)

John 8:32 famously says, "And you will know the truth, and the truth will make you free." The lessons of spiritual growth in the Bible, Swedenborg teaches, really do liberate us. The next chapter of 2 Corinthians expands on this perspective:

So we do not lose heart. Even though our outer nature is wasting away, our inner nature is being renewed day by day. For this slight momentary affliction is preparing us for an eternal weight of glory beyond all measure, because we look not at what can be seen but at what cannot be seen; for what can be seen is temporary, but what cannot be seen is eternal. (4:16–18)

As complex as the Bible can seem—repetitive, irrelevant, often obscure and arcane—Swedenborg teaches that it all comes down to the simple fundamentals of what Jesus taught to be the two greatest commandments: loving God and loving your neighbor (Matthew 22:37–40 and Mark 12:29–31). For all the complexities and tensions over differences in doctrine, Swedenborg states, it is simply following these two commandments that could—and should—unite people of all faiths. The amazing thing about the Bible is that it was written for the people of its time, but it is written for our time, too. It is every bit as relevant and applicable today as it was two thousand years ago.

> It is characteristic of the Word's style that there is something
> holy in every statement, even in every word, even at times in the
> letters themselves, so the Word unites us to the Lord and opens
> heaven. (*Sacred Scripture* §3)

Just as we know that reading a medical journal won't make us healthy, simply reading the Bible—even understanding something of its spiritual sense—won't automatically get us into heaven. It is what we do with what we know that determines if we have a healthy body. The same is true, Swedenborg teaches, for a healthy spirit.

So we should read the Bible for its influence on our lives, realizing that it is always about the person reading it. As Abraham Lincoln said, "I am busily engaged in the study of the Bible. I believe it is God's word because it finds me where I am." Reading the Bible—on both its literal and spiritual levels—helps us to learn about and know God. But just knowing him is not enough unless we use that knowledge to change the way we live and to form a meaningful relationship with him. We may "know" a friend or a spouse, but we have to learn how they think and what they love in order to build a relationship with them.

Dietrich Bonhoeffer was a German social reformer and theologian who knew something about reading the Bible and living his faith. He defied the Nazis in World War II to save Jews. And even though it went against his Christian faith, he joined in a plot to kill Hitler, who he saw as the ultimate Antichrist.

Bonhoeffer always referred to the Bible as "the *Word of God,* as though God existed and was alive and wanted to speak to us through it. The whole point of studying the text was to get to the God *behind* the text" (Metaxas 2013, 99). He rejected what he called "cheap grace," or going through the motions of believing in God but not really living your faith under duress. Although he was in great danger in Hitler's Germany, he passed up the chance to escape to America because he knew that what he was doing was right in the eyes of God. He was captured and then executed in Flossenbürg just weeks before the end of the war.

He left this powerful testament to his faith and his devotion to reading the Bible in a letter to a friend, Eberhard Bethge, written from Tegel Prison, July 21, 1944:

> Later I discovered and am still discovering up to this very
> moment that it is only by living completely in this world that
> one learns to believe. One must abandon every attempt to make
> something of oneself. . . . This is what I mean by worldliness—
> taking life in one's stride, with all its duties and problems, its
> successes and failures, its experiences and helplessnesses. It is
> in such a life that we throw ourselves utterly in the arms of God
> and participate in his sufferings in the world and watch with
> Christ in Gethsemane. That is faith.

This echoes an inspiring letter written by John Rainolds—who helped bring about the Authorized Version of the King James Bible in 1611—on the importance of reading the Bible, listening to God's teachings, and living them. A review at the end of the 1979 translation of the King James Bible concludes with this excerpt from his heartfelt letter:

> Divinity, the knowledge of God, is the water of life. God forbid
> that you should think that divinity consists of words, as a wood
> doth of trees. True divinity cannot be learned unless we frame
> our hearts and minds wholly to it. The knowledge of God must
> be learned of God. . . . We have to use two means, prayers and the
> reading of the Holy Scriptures, prayers for ourselves to talk with
> God, and reading to hear God talk with us. We must diligently
> give ourselves to reading and meditating on the Holy Scriptures.
> I pray that you may. (Rainolds 1979, 1236)

God has given us his word in the Bible to help us live good lives and draw closer to him, but we need to read it to make that connection. What it says to us comes from that still, small voice within, connecting us with each other and with God. It transcends time and space and relates to our own spiritual journeys. When we read the Bible in this way, what appears to our everyday mind and eyes as historical, worldly events and people becomes a mirror for the life of our soul. We hear the voice of God: "This is the way; walk in it" (Isaiah 30:21).

This book is just an introduction to the depth of all that was written by Swedenborg. There is much more, including teachings about life after death, divine providence, married love that continues after death, and the nature of God himself. Anyone so inclined is invited to explore further and to decide for themselves if this is a teaching that will help them learn and grow.

In one of their first encounters with Jesus, John and two other disciples asked him where he was staying, and he said to them simply, "Come and see."

The following day, Jesus went to Galilee, where he found Philip and said to him, "Follow me."

Philip then went to Nathanael and told him, "We have found him about whom Moses in the law and also the prophets wrote, Jesus son of Joseph from Nazareth."

A perplexed Nathanael asked, "Can anything good come out of Nazareth?"

Nathanael was skeptical, maybe even cynical. Jerusalem was the heart and soul of the Jewish world. The people of Nazareth were looked down upon as uneducated and unsophisticated. Good things might be expected out of Jerusalem but not out of Nazareth.

Philip's response was gentle and inviting: "Come and see" (John 1:39, 43, 45, 46).

He didn't argue. He simply was saying to Nathanael to open his mind, open his heart, be prepared to see in a new way, and have his life changed for the better.

Swedenborg teaches that God is similarly calling us to "come and see" the Bible in a whole new light. He says that if we are willing, if we open our hearts and minds to all that God is trying to teach us about living good and useful lives, and if we come to see him anew as a visible God, present with us, then we can be forever transformed.

When describing one of his experiences in the spiritual world, Swedenborg writes of visiting a temple with an inscription above the door: *Nunc Licet*, "which means that we are now allowed to use our intellect to explore the mysteries of faith" (*True Christianity* §508:3).

Come and see.

BIBLIOGRAPHY

As is customary in Swedenborgian studies, throughout this book references to Swedenborg's writings are cited by paragraph number, which were inserted by Swedenborg and are uniform across most editions and translations. Bibliographic information for the editions used in this volume are given below.

Bigelow, John. 1953. *The Bible That Was Lost and Is Found*. New York: New-Church Board of Publication.

Bonhoeffer, Dietrich. 1959. *Letters and Papers from Prison*. Edited by Eberhard Bethge. Translated by Reginald H. Fuller. New York: The Macmillan Company. Accessed online at https://archive.org/stream/ DietrichBonhoefferLettersFromPrison/Dietrich_Bonhoeffer_ Letters_from_Prison_djvu.txt.

Brown, Dan. 2009. *The Lost Symbol*. New York: Doubleday.

Browning, Elizabeth Barrett. 1917. *Aurora Leigh*. In *The Oxford Book of English Mystical Verse*, edited by D.H.S. Nicholson and A.H.E. Lee. Oxford: The Clarendon Press.

Emerson, Ralph Waldo. 1930. *Representative Men*. Boston: Houghton Mifflin.

The Holy Bible. 1979. New King James Version. Nashville, TN: Thomas Nelson, Inc.

Keller, Helen. 2011. *How I Would Help the World*. West Chester, PA: Swedenborg Foundation.

———. 1953. *My Religion*. New York: Swedenborg Foundation.

Kenyon, Frederic G., ed. 1898. *The Letters of Elizabeth Barrett Browning.* New York: Macmillan.

Lewis, C.S. 2001. *The Screwtape Letters.* New York: HarperCollins.

Metaxas, Eric. 2013. *7 Men and the Secret of Their Greatness.* Nashville, TN: Thomas Nelson, Inc.

Paine, Thomas. (1794) 2003. *The Writings of Thomas Paine—Volume 4 (1794–1796): The Age of Reason.* Accessed online at http://www.gutenberg.org/ebooks/3743.

Solzhenitsyn, Aleksandr Isayevich. 1974. *The Gulag Archipelago, 1918–1956: An Experiment in Literary Investigation.* 2 vols. New York: Harper & Row.

Swedenborg, Emanuel. (1785–89) 1994–97. *Apocalypse Explained.* 6 vols. Translated by John C. Ager. Revised by John Whitehead. 2nd edition. West Chester, PA: Swedenborg Foundation.

———. (1766) 1997. *Apocalypse Revealed.* 2 vols. Translated by John Whitehead. West Chester, PA: Swedenborg Foundation.

———. (1764) 2010. *Divine Providence.* Translated by George F. Dole. West Chester, PA: Swedenborg Foundation.

———. (1758) 2010. *Heaven and Hell.* Translated by George F. Dole. West Chester, PA: Swedenborg Foundation.

———. 1766. *Revelation Unveiled.* Forthcoming. New Century Edition. West Chester, PA: Swedenborg Foundation.

———. (1763) 2015. *Sacred Scripture / White Horse.* Translated by George F. Dole. West Chester, PA: Swedenborg Foundation.

———. (1749) 2008–12. *Secrets of Heaven.* 2 vols. Translated by Lisa Hyatt Cooper. West Chester, PA: Swedenborg Foundation.

———. 1749–56. *Secrets of Heaven.* Unpublished section translations by Lisa Hyatt Cooper. §§2117, 3195, 5972, 6476, 8455, 8593, 8604, 8606, 8943, 9229.

———. (1771) 2006–11. *True Christianity.* 2 vols. Translated by Jonathan S. Rose. West Chester, PA: Swedenborg Foundation.